Legacy
of
Magic

By the Same Author
The Magic Stone

Leonie Kooiker

Legacy
of
Magic

Illustrated by Carl Hollander

Translation from the Dutch by Patricia Crampton

William Morrow and Company
New York   1981

English translation copyright © 1981 by William Morrow and Company
Original copyright © 1979 by Leonie Kooiker, Papendrecht, The Netherlands
First published in The Netherlands under the title *Het Oerlanderboek*

Printed in the United States of America.
1 2 3 4 5 6 7 8 9 10

Library of Congress Cataloging in Publication Data

Kooiker, Leonie.
  Legacy of magic.

  Translation of: Het Oerlanderboek.
  Summary: A modern-day witch's apprentice, his skeptical friend, and an ancient book of magic come together in the course of a hunt for a hidden legacy of priceless coins.
    [1. Witchcraft—Fiction. 2. Buried treasure—Fiction] I. Hollander, Carl, ill. II. Title.
PZ7.K83557Le [Fic] 81-11013
ISBN 0-688-00721-X AACR2
ISBN 0-688-00722-8 (lib. bdg.)

Contents

Legacy of Magic

CHAPTER I

Grandpa Is Cracked

"Alec!"

"Yes, Grandpa?"

"Do you remember what I told you the other day? About that book?"

"Yes, Grandpa."

"Come and have a look. I've got it here."

Grandpa had already mentioned that book at least ten times. It had been his father's, his grandfather's, and an endless number of grandfathers' before that. It was to be Alec's one day, and now at last he was going to have a look at it.

Grandpa opened the big cupboard and took out a cardboard box. He shuffled to the table with it and went back to shut the cupboard again.

"It's a precious heirloom. I've packed it up well."

In the box was a small iron chest with a padlock. Alec thought that looked exciting. Would it be a book with

pictures? Or was it so old that it would have those deco-
rated letters in it? What a fuss Grandpa was making over
his bunch of keys!

The book was smaller than Alec had imagined. It had
curly edges and was covered in black leather. Grandpa
lifted it very gently out of the chest. Alec could see that
there were more books and papers inside. Now Grandpa
was opening the book. What peculiar letters! They looked
like Chinese. Alec could not read them.

"What does it say?" he asked.

"I think you could learn a lot from it," said Grandpa.

"Can you read it?"

Grandpa shook his head sadly. "No, I can't. I never
learned the old tongue, but that's why I'm giving you the
book now. I was twenty-three when my father gave it to
me. I didn't feel like bothering with it then. I regretted it
later, and now it's too late. But you're still young. You
learn easily. You got an A in Dutch, didn't you? And you
already know some English, too. If you do your very best
at school and go on learning later, you can get a lot of
pleasure out of this book."

Alec was deeply disappointed. He wanted to get some
pleasure out of the book right now. And instead of that he
had to learn Chinese first! Grandpa had not felt like learning it himself once. Well, Alec did not feel like it either.
Grandpa could keep his silly book. But Alec dared not say
so.

Now Grandpa was taking another book out of the little
chest. This one looked still older, if possible.

"This little book is over two hundred years old. An Alec Aulder transcribed whole passages of it in 1761. Look, there are the same strange letters written here, and here is the translation on the opposite page."

"Then you *do* know what's in the book?"

"A little. Not really, because I can't understand it. Here, for instance: this bit is about a friend. First it tells you how to find a friend and then how to cook him. That can't be right. And it's like that all the way through. It's a very odd book. That's why I put it to one side in the past. I thought it must be one of great-grandfather's jokes. But it's no joke. It's . . . I think I'd better tell you more about it another time."

Grandpa replaced the battered book from 1761 in the chest, laid the black leather book on top of it, and closed the lid. Alec hadn't even held the book. Chest into box, box into cupboard, cupboard locked, and the tinkling bunch of keys back in Grandpa's baggy trouser pocket. Well, Grandpa had no reason to fear that Alec was going to take a stealthy look at the book. He had better things to do.

What things?

Alec lived in Amsterdam, and during vacation he was always glad to go and stay with his grandfather in the little Dutch village close to the German frontier. He was hardly ever bored, although everything was quite different from home. You couldn't go swimming or play soccer or visit the library. You just had to wait and see if anything happened, and on the whole it was fun. Once he had seen a calf being born and a weasel running off with a mouse.

Sometimes he was allowed to go and help hay or milk cows for one of the farmers. Quite often he helped with the real work, which was fine. But now and again he found everything dull and drab. Then he liked to think of himself as the boy from the big city, someone who was familiar with things they had never heard of down here. Grandpa and his book! Had he any idea how many books there were in the shops in Amsterdam?

Alec left the house and strode across the untidy little front yard, making for the road. There was no traffic, just a couple of bicyclists in the distance, probably people from one of the summer cottages near the castle. To the left was the village: a church, a café, the school, and six shops. And to the right you passed the castle, but it had gone to pot; it was just a shabby building where no one lived. You would have to come from a backward little spot like this to call it a castle at all.

The bicyclists rode slowly past. Alec thought of the crowds at home: the rattling trams and abusive drivers. Even a little old woman whom he sometimes saw walking to the stores was in more of a hurry than the people here. No one in Amsterdam would ever think of learning Chinese in order to read an old book he happened to own. Grandpa was funny, really quite cracked!

Along the roadside there were daisies and buttercups and a whole lot of plants whose names Alec did not know. Among them were grasshoppers and fat caterpillars and beetles. When Alec had nothing else to do he went hunting for creatures. He had actually once seen a salamander.

"Hello!"

A high, ramshackle lady's bike appeared, and on it rode a boy with a strange, old-fashioned basket: Chris.

"Hello."

They had met only once before, in the village shop where both of them had been sent to buy tobacco, Alec for Grandpa, of course, and Chris for an old woman called Janna. She lived in the middle of the woods and smoked a pipe. Chris had told Alec that he came from The Hague, and he spent every vacation in the village, but he hadn't said how Janna was related to him or why he came to see her all the time.

"Has Janna finished the tobacco already?" asked Alec.

"No," said Chris, "the salt."

"Did you have to ride all the way to the village just for salt?"

"Yes, I felt like it."

Chris had dismounted and was walking beside Alec, pushing the old bike. The basket swung from the handlebars.

"My grandpa is cracked," said Alec.

"How? Does he say the same thing three times over? Or does he get under the shower with his umbrella up?"

"No, not like that."

"You know, my grandmother is quite normal, very nice and certainly not cracked. But I know two old women who certainly are sort of crazy, and you can have a great time with them. I mean, being a little nutty may not be so bad. It can really be fun."

"My grandpa has a very old book, which I'm supposed

to have later on. That's what he said, at least, but now he wants me to learn Chinese first, so that I can read it."

"Is it a Chinese book?"

"No, but it's funny-looking sign writing. Anyway, I'm not going to read it. It's about a friend you have to cook, Grandpa says. Cracked!"

"Perhaps it's a book of spells."

"Well, so?"

"If I had a book like that, I'd want to read it. I'd learn the signs. Just imagine, a book of spells! You could have a whole lot of fun with that."

"There are no such things as spells."

"I know that, but all the same it's fun to know how to do them."

"Not for me."

Chris got back on his bike. "I'm going to buy my salt. 'Bye."

" 'Bye."

Alec went on walking along the roadside. Spells! Chris was cracked too. The crickets with their little chirping sounds were saying the same thing. Alec began to sing, "Crackpot, crackpot, how many daisies have you got?"

Were daisies really as white as snow? Flowers were never dirty. Buttercups, for instance, were much yellower than butter. Wasn't there a single one with a slightly paler color?

"Daisies are yellow, buttercups white, Grandpa and Chris are cracked all right," Alec sang aloud. Now if I see a white buttercup, I've made a magic spell, he thought.

"Daisies are yel—"

There was a yellow daisy.

When he came closer, Alec could see that it was not really a daisy but a flower that looked very much like one.

Of course.

But it *was* an extraordinary coincidence.

CHAPTER II

Ants

There was food growing in Grandpa's backyard: potatoes to be dug, beets to be pulled, and spinach to be cut. Every morning they found something to pick together. Grandpa would cook it, and Alec would set the table. When they were eating the beets that had still been growing only yesterday, Alec began to talk about the book.

"How old is it actually, Grandpa?"

"Very old. It was always copied again when the paper had almost worn through."

"Doesn't it say the year anywhere?"

"The years were counted in a different way then."

"Oh, how funny! Probably a Chinese way. Or isn't it Chinese? What are those letters anyhow?"

"I don't know, Alec. I ought to send it away to find out what language it is, to some university or somewhere, but I'm not allowed to let it out of my hands."

"Who doesn't let you? It's no use to you like this. The book is no use to anyone."

"Perhaps it will be some use to you later on, if you learn the language."

Alec quickly popped a big piece of potato in his mouth. When it was finished, he knew exactly what to say. "How could I? I don't know what language it is."

Grandpa laughed. "You'll find out, boy. As long as you're interested. At least you've started to talk about it yourself. I was beginning to be afraid that you couldn't be bothered with it, like your father, and that seemed a shame."

"I want to know a whole lot of languages, because later I may be a traveler and it's easier when you can talk to everybody. But I'm not going to learn a whole language just for one book."

"That was just what I used to think about it—exactly that. Quite understandable that you should say that, and sensible too! Yes, just make a start with English. That will be most useful to you for the time being. Yes, forget about the book. Later on we shall see if it's going to mean anything to you or not."

Alec would have liked to ask more about the business of the cooked friend, but Grandpa got up to beat the eggs. They finished with an omelette every day, because that was what both of them liked best. Alec took the dirty plates to the kitchen. I'll ask him later, while we're washing the dishes, he thought. But his grandfather kept on chatting about shoes and ships and sealing wax, as the saying goes, and nothing came of it.

Grandpa had told him to forget the book. Alec had no plans to read it, yet he thought about it all the time.

Grandpa was cunning not to have let him see it properly and also not to let him talk about it anymore.

"Later, when you're a bit older, boy."

When Alec was two days older, they were looking for mushrooms together in the woods. Grandpa got a little breathless and sat down on the edge of a ditch to rest. He sat in silence, looking at a big frond of bracken through which the sun was shining.

"Alec!"

"Yes, Grandpa?"

"Do you see how beautiful that is? Just look at the way that leaf grows. And the color. Green-gold."

"Yes, Grandpa."

Grandpa sighed.

"Alec, listen a moment."

Alec sighed too, but only a little, because he was really fond of his grandfather. Old people could not help becoming a little bit tedious.

"When you are as old as I am, over seventy, things can end suddenly. I may not live much longer, and there is something you have to know."

Alec sat down beside his grandfather. He watched a procession of ants walking in a long line under the bracken.

"I hadn't intended to talk about the book anymore this summer, but I have to tell you how it was that I became interested in it, although I had never cared about it before."

Two ants were busy dealing with a dead fly.

"You know we once used to live by the river?"

"Yes, in the house that burned down."

"Exactly. It was a big, old house. The whole family could easily have lived in the kitchen alone. There was a wooden attic above it, and the book was in an old cupboard up there."

The ants, carrying their fly, had reached a dead branch. They could not hoist it over the branch. Another one joined in to help. Grandpa kept falling silent. You could see that he was thinking very old thoughts.

"I didn't have that little iron chest then. The book and everything connected with it were wrapped in a linen cloth. I never looked at it, and when the house was burned I did not even miss it."

Alec had often heard tales from those days. A friend of his father had been involved in it all, and he told very amusing stories: how Grandmother had rushed out of the house in her nightgown, carrying the rarest thing she owned, an umbrella stand made of an elephant's foot. It was still around, stuffed away somewhere in Alec's house. He had seen it once and thought it dirty and creepy.

Grandpa shifted his position cautiously. "There was a schoolmaster there who was interested in runes and other old writings, and I promised to get the book down from the attic for him sometime. I forgot three times, and the day after I took it to him an airplane full of fire bombs fell on our garden. Quite extraordinary."

Alec saw that the ants were biting the dead fly into

pieces. That was what people had done with the elephant. A whole elephant was too heavy to take home. It had been cut up, and Grandma's uncle had received one foot.

"But that wasn't what I wanted to say," Grandpa continued. Alec looked at him. He had been listening a little, but not very much. It didn't matter. The important point must be coming later.

"The schoolmaster studied it thoroughly, although he didn't know the letters either, but he did discover a few of them with the help of the 1761 translation. There's still some writing of his in the chest."

Alec's thoughts began to wander again. Grandpa had not yet reached the important part of his story.

"There was a passage in it about the moon and the stars. I can't remember exactly what it said, but I can look it up. In any case, what it boiled down to was the time of the new moon in August, and then there was something about Mars. According to this man, it was an unusual situation, something that happens only once every so many hundred years. And on that day, or in fact that night, the book had to be taken away from the house by the river. The book said so: it was not allowed to be in the house by the river. And I had done what had to be done, although I did not know it. At that time we were much too busy to think about it. The war was still on, and the schoolmaster moved to some relations'. But I didn't forget, and to me it proved the value of the book. Later I discovered that there were a lot more things of that kind in it. It is a very special book, Alec. The kind of heirloom that no one else has. And that is what I wanted to tell you."

"Oh," said Alec, feeling dreadfully ashamed. He had been watching the ants. They had not left a single fragment of the dead fly. Meanwhile, Grandpa had told the important part of his story, and he, Alec, had paid no attention. What *had* Grandpa been saying? Something about stars and the house by the river. And the schoolmaster had moved somewhere else. Somewhere else, he had heard that. But what was it all about? He did not know. Grandpa was sitting there so calmly, no longer out of breath, but he was very old. He had wanted to tell Alec something before he died. But he wasn't going to die yet, was he? If he thought carefully, Alec ought to be able to ask a clever question to find out what Grandpa had meant. He could not actually say, "I wasn't listening." That would be much too hard on Grandpa. And having the story begin again from the beginning would be no fun, either.

"We had better go on," said Grandpa. "I've had a nice rest now. Where's the basket?"

"I'm carrying it, Grandpa."

And off they went together, in their usual way. They had walked side by side like this when he was only two years old. Alec had never had an argument with his grandpa.

CHAPTER III

Castle

What fun it would be to see Chris again. Where did Janna actually live? In the woods, but they were very big.

"Grandpa, do you know where Janna lives?"

"Janna? That depends who you mean. I think there must be ten or twenty Jannas living here. The women are called Janna, or Hanna, Mina, Dina, or Dika."

"She lives in the woods and she smokes a pipe."

"Nobody lives in the woods. You must mean on the edge of the woods. A pipe? That's something I've never seen, a woman with a pipe. What does she look like?"

Alec did not know. "She's quite old, I think. But she really does live here, Grandpa. In the middle of the woods. Chris told me so himself."

"Nobody lives in the woods. There isn't even a path."

There certainly were scarcely any paths. Wherever there was enough room for them, young saplings were growing up between the old ones that had fallen. In the sparsely grown patches they hunted for mushrooms, and not until they went home did Alec see a path with the clear marks of bicycle wheels. If nobody except Chris knew where Janna lived, he was the one who had bicycled along there. So it would be quite easy to find the house. Without asking his grandfather anymore, Alec decided to have a look for himself. He did so the next day.

Alec had no bicycle with him, so he set off immediately after breakfast. It was a ten-minute walk to the castle. Beyond it lay a farm and a strip of woodland, with summer cottages. Yesterday he and his grandfather had taken at least half an hour to reach the spot, and things did not go much faster today. But he found the path with the wheel tracks at once. They looked just as fresh as they had yesterday. Did no one ever walk this way?

The little path made a wide arc and then curved in the other direction. There were no side paths, and the trees in the woods were all very alike. The track vanished quite soon, but Alec kept on, and now and again he came across a little patch of sand or a half-squashed clump of grass where you could see that a narrow bicycle wheel had passed.

As he walked along, hearing neither birds nor wind, Alec thought that this was the first time in his life that he had been so far away from anyone. In the city there were people everywhere, and here he had never gone on a real walk on his own.

"Now I am completely alone," he said aloud. The feeling was a new one, a nice one. Farther on, past some aromatic pines, he could see young birch trees and thin, dry, feathery grass.

There was a crow sitting in a tree. It watched Alec so intelligently that for a minute he was not alone, but the crow flew off and then he could feel the loneliness.

In another moment he could no longer follow the way clearly. Bicycle tracks had not appeared for some time. There were few trees, and the ground was dry. You could walk straight on, left, or somewhere in between. Only on the right-hand side was there some thicker growth, but even between the heather and the broom he could make his way without difficulty.

Perhaps the house where Chris was staying was close by now. If he tied his handkerchief to something he could go on a little farther to look around. But perhaps Chris was not there anymore. Then he would find only the old woman with the pipe, and Alec was not certain that it would be fun to bump into someone like that unexpectedly. He probably would find her difficult to understand. He always had difficulty with the dialect of the people here, especially when they were old. And then Alec suddenly knew for certain, If I go on, I shall get lost.

He said, "I won't do it," and turned on his heel.

Everyone knows that the way back from a place always looks different from the way to a place, and when there's not even a real path, it's more difficult than ever. Alec soon realized that he was lost. All the trees were strange, there was not a flower or a plant that he'd seen before, and he had no idea which way to go to find the path again. He could see no trace of a bicycle wheel or of his own footprints.

A quarter of an hour before, Alec had been alone for the first time. Now he really was alone, for then no one else had known where he was, but now *he* no longer knew himself. Meanwhile, he went on walking, in the direction he thought led back, where there were more and taller trees. He looked at the sun and tried to remember on which side of Grandpa's little house it was at this time of day. What time of day *was* it? And could you really find your direction that way? Or not?

Alec said, "I'm lost, and it's no fun!"

Then he heard something, a familiar squeaking sound: Chris on Janna's old bike. And he saw something moving between the trees.

Oh, *there* was the path!

"Hi, Chris."

"Hello. What are you doing here?"

"I wanted to look you up, but I couldn't find Janna's house."

"Right. No one can find it. Janna doesn't like visitors much."

"Except you, of course?"

"Except me." Chris looked quite content and did not talk about how tiresome Janna could be. She had lived alone for more than thirty years, speaking to no one. Sometimes she could not stand having Chris there. Then she would think up an errand for him, and he could stay away most of the day. Today he had to buy a box of matches, and he had thought at once that it would be fun to look Alec up, because Alec had a grandfather with a book of spells, and Chris was very keen indeed to see it. All things magical interested Chris, since he had found a magic stone the year before and been chosen to learn the magic arts from old Janna. For Janna was a witch.

"Shall we go and do something together?"

"Fine."

Alec saw that the path did not go at all the way he had thought. He stayed close behind the bicycle and was ready to do anything Chris suggested, as long as it was not hide-and-seek.

"Will your grandfather mind if I come?"

"To us? In Grandpa's cottage? But nothing's there."

"Perhaps we could help him with something. I'm always helping Janna."

Alec helped Grandpa too: in the garden, preparing food, even helping to build a birdhouse. Grandpa was not very handy, and Alec was always quicker to see how it should be done, but he never showed it. He could not imagine that he would find it enjoyable to have Chris there. "I'd rather go somewhere else."

"Fine with me. We can go and look at the castle."

"Can we? It's not a museum. Do you know someone who has the key?"

"The farmer who lives next door has it, but I know how you can get in without a key." Chris was patient. He thought, First we'll do what Alec wants. Grandpa and the book will have to come later.

"I'd like to see it," said Alec.

"That's what I thought."

The woodland path came out beside the farm. There were two dogs, which started barking like crazy, but luckily they were behind a fence. The castle was set in a big park surrounded by a wall, but the wall had broken down in some places and from the woods you could come out on the drive that ran around the building. The park had once been very beautiful but was now dark and threatening, for the trees had not been cut back for years and the bushes below them had run wild. Right in front of the castle was a rusty gate. It was impossible to open the gate anymore, but people who wanted to go into the woods simply walked around it, because it was shorter that way than past the farm. A narrow path had developed. Chris did not go to that path but hid his bike under a privet bush and went toward the back of the castle. A terrace was there with a low wall around it. A gray flowerpot stood at each corner.

Chris climbed on the wall to a window that he could push up. Alec could still hear the dogs barking. He crawled quickly in beside Chris and closed the window again. They were standing in a high room. In it was a pale brown marble fireplace set in dark wooden paneling.

Alec asked, "Is there a secret chamber?"

"I don't think so. This isn't a medieval castle, just a big old house. It's not very interesting, you know. There's nothing left inside."

They came into a wide hallway and looked at the front

rooms. They were all paneled in wood as well. Alec knocked on the paneling. It would be fun if one of the panels turned out to be a door! There was a dark adjoining room and behind it two kitchens, where the air smelled moldy. The pump creaked but gave no water. Back to the hallway. Chris was right. There was nothing to be seen. *Clump, clump* on the wooden stairs.

Chris called, "Eeee-yow!" The sound echoed through the empty space.

"Don't make all that noise!"

"It doesn't matter. The farmer never comes here and particularly not in the summer when he's so busy."

Chris stamped ahead. Alec followed, feeling less at ease.

"Look, here's the bathroom."

In it there was still a bathtub, with claw feet, and over the edge of the tub hung a pair of jeans.

"Hey," said Chris, "someone has been here after all."

Much more gently he pushed open the door to the next room. In the corner, under the window, lay a sleeping bag and an old blanket. There were a couple of empty beer bottles, a plastic shopping bag, and half a sandwich.

"There's someone living here."

Alec thought it was high time to be going. Chris did not. He went over to the sleeping bag and had a good look at everything. "Do you think this belongs to a man?"

"Yes."

"Women can drink beer too."

"They can have fleas too."

Chris took a step backward. "Let's look around every-

where, in the closets and the attic. Perhaps there's something or someone somewhere else as well."

Alec was not convinced, but if Chris really wanted to and went first, okay. They found nothing and no one. The big rooms on the upper floor, the little ones in the attic, all were empty, dusty, with blistered paint and peeling paper. One little room upstairs was locked.

"Bluebeard's chamber."

"It must be."

The pleasure of the search began to fade. There were so many closets and all so completely empty. They decided to leave and clattered down the hallways and stairs to the big garden room to climb out of the window again. This time Alec went first.

CHAPTER IV

The Book

"Quiet," said Chris suddenly.

His hand already on the copper knob of the window lock, Alec stopped.

"There's someone at the back door," whispered Chris.

A heavy thud echoed through the empty house. They tiptoed back to peep through a crack in the doorway to the hall, but before they reached it they heard someone already on the stairs.

"Wait until he's upstairs, and then we'll go, okay?"

Plonk, plonk, plonk.

"It *is* a man, that's for sure."

Very cautiously they opened the door. *Creep, creep,* right against the wall, as far as the stairs, and then they froze, for something came rolling down, an apple. And another and another. Someone above, a man, said, "Damn!" And a paper bag was thrown after the apples in a crumpled ball. The boys were already back in the garden room. Alec had quickly snatched up an apple.

They went on looking through the crack.

"Is he coming back?" asked Alec.

"Can't hear anything. Come on, let's collect apples."

Back to the hallway . . . one apple . . . two. "There he comes!" Another hasty flight. They waited, holding their breath, listening for steps.

"We don't really have to run away," whispered Chris. "He has just as little right here as we have. At least I can't believe that he is the owner of this house."

"It might be someone who's come to fix the place up."

"A carpenter or a painter. Yes, possible, but I don't think so."

"I think he's up to something sneaky. He's a villain, and we're on his trail. So far he doesn't know, and he mustn't know either, because we want to find out what villainous things he's up to."

"He's a murderer, of course, and the body is in Bluebeard's chamber."

"Oh, yes, of course. He's come to get it."

"Yes, he hid it upstairs for the time being to get rid of it, and now he's going to bury it in the woods before it stinks the house up."

"Great, a real murderer."

"I can't hear anything in the hallway. He must be staying upstairs."

"But," said Alec, throwing the core of his apple to the place where the hearth should have been, "if he is going to be carrying a body, he may just stay there eating apples until nighttime, and I've no intention of waiting here all that time. What time is it now?"

"It's nearly half-past twelve."

"Then Grandpa will have set the table."

They looked at each other. "Does he get cross if you're late?"

"Not a bit," said Alec, but he looked worried. At home he didn't mind being late at all, even if his mother grumbled, but Grandpa was used to eating at exactly half-past twelve. He had brought in some radishes from the garden again, and Alec thought it would be too bad if he had to sit down alone at a table with two plates on it. He found it impossible to explain to Chris.

Chris understood anyway. "We'll go at once," he said. "You can come on the back of the bike. I'll wait till you're finished, and then we'll decide what to do later on."

Naturally he had no intention of being left alone in the gloomy house either.

"I'm sure Grandpa would be glad to have you eat with us," said Alec.

The window squeaked when they pushed it open. They jumped out quickly and saw at once that there was a bicycle leaning against the wall, a bicycle painted bright yellow.

"Look at that! We'll be able to recognize it again!"

They preferred not to think that a murderer might perhaps use a less striking means of transport if he were in the midst of hiding a body. They dragged their own bicycle out of the bushes and wriggled it past the old gate. Chris began to pedal so hard that Alec, behind him, was afraid the old rattletrap of a bike would give up. Jolting and wobbling, they reached the cottage.

"Quick, wasn't it?" said Chris.

"First class deluxe."

Grandpa was not even growing impatient. "So, boy, turned up with a friend, have you? That's nice."

Alec had to set another place. Chris watched Grandpa as he cut neat sandwiches. He had silky white hair and long, thin hands with brown freckles on them. His coat was too wide. You could see that he had been fatter once. He sat at the table in silence, looking kindly. Alec was silent too, because he didn't want to say that he had been lost, or that they had been inside the castle. Chris wrestled with the cheese slicer and chopped his radishes in thin slices the way Alec's grandfather did. At home he popped radishes in his mouth whole. Different people had different customs. Chris had known that for a long time, and it was generally best to behave like the people you were with, especially if you wanted something from them. The moment had come to ask about the book. What was the best way to set about it?

Help clear away first, of course—lid on the butter dish, saucer over the radishes, plates to the kitchen.

"Oh, no, boys, I'll wash up on my own. You go off and play."

"Shall we go and see if the yellow bike is still there?" asked Alec.

"No, let's stay here. It's so cozy here."

"Oh." Alec looked quite surprised, and Chris had to laugh.

"Oh, well. What I really— Would you ask your grandfather whether I could see the book?"

Alec looked more surprised than ever. "That book? But there's nothing to see."

"But old books happen to be my very greatest hobby. And even if I'm not allowed to read it I would be very glad if your grandfather would tell us something about it."

"I haven't even seen it properly myself."

"I showed you the castle, and with a murderer in it too. Now you can come up with that book."

"Okay. I'll ask."

Grandpa was messing around in the kitchen. They could hear tinkling sounds and a drawer being pulled out. Then he came in with a tray.

"So, young fellows, still here?"

"Grandpa, may Chris see the old book?"

Grandpa put the tray on the table and looked from one to the other. "Why?"

"Because Chris's hobby happens to be old books," said Alec.

"Because it's so old," said Chris. "People from long, long ago have had it in their hands. And I should very much like to see the writing. I looked at a book once that was written by monks. I'd like to know if it looks like that."

"No, monks had nothing to do with it."

Grandpa began to clear away the knives and forks one by one, and *shuffle shuffle shuff* he took the plates to the plate cupboard and the glasses to the glass cupboard. And then he said, "There's nothing against bringing it out."

They stood close behind him as he turned the key.

"Go and sit at the table. Are your hands clean?"

And then the routine took place all over again: the box, the little iron chest, and the black book that had disappointed Alec so much.

"Grandpa," asked Alec, "what was that again that you were saying about the schoolmaster?"

"You mean about the prophecy?"

"Are there prophecies in the book?" asked Chris, impressed.

"Prophecies, history, magic, everything. Even mathematics, so I've heard. But I'm bound to add that I know nothing about it."

"What sort of history? How long ago?"

"The history of Auldland. You know our name is Aulder. That means that we came from Auldland originally, but nobody knows where it is or where it has gone. I think it might have been in North Holland, a part that vanished in the floods. The word *sunk* is in the book. Auldland sank, and the Aulders who survived had to make sure that their knowledge was not lost. It's here in this book, the knowledge of Auldland, and yet it has been lost after all. I am too old, Alec's father had no time for it and has never been interested. Alec is too young. The interest may come one day, but it doesn't look much like it."

"Oh," said Chris, "what a shame I'm not an Aulder!"

Grandpa laughed.

"Would you let me hold it, please?"

Alec felt that Chris was overdoing it. Grandpa gave him the book and watched tensely. Chris turned over a few pages with great care, while Alec took the other book from

1761 out of the little chest. If you wanted to know anything about it, you needed that one. That at least looked
a little bit like a normal book.

"Look," said Grandpa, "this is the word for Auldland,
and here it is again. The schoolmaster made a vocabulary
list for it. And this is the sun, this whole passage is about
the sun. They needed only one letter to write the word
sun."

Alec began to turn the pages of the book. Then he
wanted to know how to write sun in Auldish and looked
over Chris's shoulder.

"Now this is one of the extraordinary things," said
Grandpa. "It says here that there are other suns and that
everything turns around each other, and yet this book is
from an earlier time than the books of the monks."

"How do you know that?"

"It says so here. That's what they said, the people who
knew about these things. Come, let me pack it up again
now. You've had a good look, haven't you? What do you
think of it?"

"Terrific," said Chris. "If it was mine, I would look at it
every day until I could read everything in it."

"Yes, yes, but it is difficult," said Grandpa, replacing the
book in the iron chest with the schoolmaster's writing.
Snap went the lock, and Alec noticed that he still had the
other book in his hand.

"Grandpa . . ."

"Yes, next time. I will tell you some more, but not now.
Next time."

Grandpa was already on his way to the cupboard with the heavy box.

Fair enough, thought Alec, next time. He held the book behind his back. Now upstairs, quickly!

And while Chris was saying a polite thank-you, Alec ran quickly up to the little room where he always slept and hid the book under his pillow. No, not there, under the mattress, safer still. Tonight he would look at it again in peace. Perhaps the prophecy was actually in this book. That was odd. Grandpa had not talked of a prophecy when they were in the woods together. And by now he had learned a little sense. Grandpa really did behave rather oddly about that book. Alec had thought so from the first, and he thought so now. First showing it and then suddenly snap, away with the book, *lock, lock, lock.* As if there were a thief behind every door. Grandpa was too soft an old man to give a thief much trouble. If the book was so valuable, he shouldn't keep it in the house. Crackbrain, crackbrain, wrong or right again?

He walked into the room again, whistling.

"Coming, Chris? I'll pedal the bike this time."

Would the murderer still be in the castle? Would the yellow bike still be standing there?

CHAPTER V

Magic

The room where the sleeping bag was, the murderer's room, was at the front of the house. So instead of going by way of the gate, where they could be seen from the window, the boys bicycled past it and took the longer way to the farm, with the dark, angry dogs, so that they would arrive at the back of the house. The yellow bicycle was no longer there.

"Shall we go in?"

"Naturally. Just see if the back door is open."

"Yes, it's open. We didn't even try it this morning. Perhaps we didn't need to climb through the window in that complicated way."

Chris strode in as if the house were his own, but Alec had the feeling that a big, dangerous man might be going to jump out of every corner.

"So you think thieves are afraid of other thieves?"

"If you're a thief by profession, you mustn't be afraid of anything."

"I'm not going to be a thief later on. Are you?"

"I don't think so, but I do want to be rich."

They went first to the bathroom. The jeans were still hanging there just as before, but there was more to see in the front room. There were four beer bottles now and a carton of yoghurt, a small bag of tomatoes, half a loaf of brown bread, and a jar of peanut butter. There was also a folding chair, two maps of the district, and one or two books. One was in English and the cover showed a pale girl with a knife in her heart.

"That's his textbook," said Chris.

"It looks as if he's going to stay here."

"I must have a good look at the maps to see if there is a mark or a cross anywhere."

Alec took a look around. He was beginning to feel some sympathy for the man who had crept, with a bottle of beer and a book, into this little corner of such an enormously big, abandoned house.

"Can't see anything suspicious," said Chris.

"Let's go out again. I think this is a dreary den. If I were a tramp I would much rather sleep under the trees somewhere than here, especially in this beautiful weather."

Chris also thought it would be a good idea to go. "We haven't got anything to pick the lock of the little room with, so we'll just have to go back for something."

"Right."

They pushed the bicycle over the crumbling old wall and left it lying there, because they wanted to stay in the woods.

"We're police and we're supposed to be looking for a murderer," said Chris.

"He's probably hiding in the woods."

"Yes, he's probably hiding in the woods."

"And up to now there have been no clues, but we're going to comb the woods."

"I've got a clue. A bicycle has been ridden through here."

"That was you."

"Oh, yes. Too bad. Let's look for footprints then. What size do you think? Twelve? He clomped so heavily on the stairs."

"Okay, we'll comb the woods until we find footprints, size eleven or twelve, but we'll have to be well armed, of course."

"I've got an automatic pistol."

There were a lot of useful weapons lying under a dead oak tree. Each of them found a crooked branch that lay comfortably against the shoulder and had a straight barrel to fire with: machine guns. Under the pines they found plenty of cones. Sometimes they slipped silently as snakes through the jungle. Then again they shouted wildly, "Pow, pow, pow," and stormed a helpless larch tree or attacked a thick bush that might pass as a robber's den. The woods were full of murderers, if you had eyes to see them.

Later they had to lie silently in ambush, because constantly pursuing someone is very tiring, so the villain had to be given a chance to walk by, unsuspecting. Chris began to talk about the book again.

"What was that about the schoolmaster's prophecy?"

"No idea," said Alec. "Grandpa told me the whole story, but I didn't pay much attention."

What an ass! thought Chris. What an everlasting, stupid ass. He said, "That book doesn't mean anything to you, does it? Why is that?"

"Oh, it was all so long ago. What good can it possibly be now? But it's partly because of Grandpa. He only tells you half of anything. He lets you see the whole for a moment, and then he can't put it away quickly enough."

"But that means there's something special about it. That's just what I think is so marvelous."

"Yes, perhaps. But if it's too difficult for Grandpa, I can't understand it either. There is some math in it. I get enough of that at school! And about the sun turning, well, that's in so many books. I don't have to read it for that."

Chris gave a sigh. What interested him most was the magic, but he could not talk to Alec about that. "And the history and the information about Auldland?"

"No interest."

Chris leaned lazily against the root of a tree thickly grown with moss. In his pocket his hand was moving over a matchbox. He turned it over and over. He could push it open with one finger. There was a little stone inside. He stood up with a jerk. He must stop before he went any further.

"It's time to go back to Janna."

Alec was disappointed. They had been having such a good game.

"It's not time to eat yet by a long shot."

"Teatime," said Chris, laughing. "Janna always makes herb tea, something different every day. I can't ask you back because she doesn't like me to."

"You had to buy matches, didn't you?"

"Look." Chris showed him the matchbox he had with him, but of course without opening it. The errands Janna sent him on were meaningless. He had to go back to the place where the bicycle was hidden, and he and Alec walked there together.

"I'll come again if you like. We have to open Bluebeard's lock with a bit of wire, don't we?"

"We'll see."

Alec trudged home alone, trying to work out for himself why he was so irritable. When he had to go home suddenly at half-past twelve, Chris had not been at all annoyed. Chris couldn't help it that Janna didn't like visitors. Janna—what was Chris to her? Not a grandson. A nephew? He must ask sometime. And then Alec knew what he found irritating—the mystery. A house that no one could find, an old woman with a pipe and herb tea, a witch. Chris had better look out. You could cook up some funny things with herbs. Alec's irritability turned slowly into a vague disquiet. He was lucky he had gotten lost this morning.

Then he was home. Grandpa was making tea as well, ordinary tea that came from a black-and-gold tin and was steeped in a brown earthenware teapot by the steaming kettle.

After supper they played cards together, and another

game, and another. It was getting late and was nearly
dark when Alec went to bed. He did give a thought to the
book under his mattress, but he did not look at it. Later.

And Chris bumped home along the woodland path. The
sunbeams threw diagonal stripes between the trees. He
heard the trilling song of a small songbird and further off
a cuckoo. Otherwise everything was quiet. No sounds of
traffic reached the wood, though you might sometimes
hear the hum of an airplane. When he reached the place
where he had seen Alec he met a crow.

"Hi, William," said Chris. The crow was one of Janna's
trained ones.

"Kra," said William, flying on toward a small fir tree.
Then Chris saw the bicycle. The yellow bike was just
lying there, flat on the ground. Nobody was there, nor
were there any size twelve footprints. Chris dismounted
and called, "Hello! Hello!"

No answer. Even the birds were silent. He looked at
the bike from all angles: no name, not even a mark.
Painted over probably. A bicycle always had a number,
but Chris had no notebook or pen to write it down,
and now that Alec was not there it did not seem to him
so necessary to play detective. He left the bike where
it was and went on.

"Where have you been?" asked Janna. "What have
you been doing?"

"I've seen the magic book, Janna."

"Humbug!"

"It looked perfectly genuine. Old as the hills. Written in runes. I know what runes look like."

"Did you have it in your hands?"

"For a minute."

"Hm."

"There's something in it, Alec says, about cooking a friend."

"Rottentooth."

"What?"

"Rottentooth. When we speak of a friend, we always mean rottentooth. It looks like moss, but it's a fungus. You have to drink the decoction, then you find out where something is. However far away it is, you will find it. The only trick is to find the rottentooth. It grows on bare tree roots, and if it doesn't want to be found, you may step on it but you won't see it. A lot of preparation is necessary and that is why it is called "friend." Rottentooth is not a nice name; if you look for that, you will never find it. You have to look for a friend, a lovely, good friend. But it's easier to look for the thing you have lost right away."

"It's the same with everything you teach me, Janna. You have to look for one herb while it's raining, another afterward, and then the moon has to be full too, or not quite, and you never know for sure if it's working."

"That's quite right. It's an art. You shouldn't embark on it for comfort. And if you don't know for certain that it's working, it certainly won't work. Did you bring the pimpernel with you?"

"Not yet. I'm going to look for it now."

"Remember, when the sun is behind the stable it will be too late."

"I'll go right away. My tea first."

"Saint-John's-wort tea, it will clear your head. And you need it when you're looking for pimpernels. There are many more behind the castle than there are here."

"There's someone living in the castle."

"Not true. If there were, I should know. It's all humbug."

"He's a tramp or something. He's moved in with a folding chair and a sleeping bag."

"Well, well, a book of magic and someone in the castle. I knew very well that something was going to happen. Didn't I say so this morning?"

"You said, 'Chris, you must go into the village again today and then get some pimpernel for me at once.'"

"Well, I did say that. You had to go to the village because something was going to happen. That's why you had to go to the village. A lot more things are going to happen. Keep your eyes open."

CHAPTER VI

Powers

The neighbor's cock crowed, a hoarse answer came from a distance, and then Grandpa's started. His cock had the best voice of all; it sounded as if it were sitting right beside Alec's ear. Under the open window, in the gutter, the sparrows were busy, and behind, in the little yard, Grandpa was busy with a pail. He must be going to water his little garden. Alec could get up and help to carry water. He could equally well stay where he was, in bed. He had been so late last night. If he were to come down now, Grandpa was sure to say, "Early to bed tonight." Alec scrabbled under his mattress. Where was that book? If he pulled it out, it would break up, of course; it was all delicate and crumbling, being two hundred years old. He got out of bed to take it out.

The text was written by hand, probably with a goose quill, he thought; the ink was brown and the paper was finely ribbed. There was his own name!

"Being gone for my lyfe's sake to Kirk, where the pious thirst for my blood, I, Alyck Aulder, shall keep these lines fast, being the hystory and the teaching of our forefathers and of all those who be come from across the water from the Auldland."

He had to read it through again: Being gone to church to save his life? Then had great-grandfather Alyck Aulder been a heretic? But surely the period of religious persecution had been much earlier than 1761?

He turned over a few pages. The paper was hard and stiff.

"This Auldland was the land across the sea, where the fludde drowned it with every stick and stone and the people who trafficked there, save for those who sailed out to sea and those who sail up to Heaven, for the Aulders were possessed of these arts, having the knowledge of rysing up in their shippes and thus removing themselves above this worlde. When that these plagues and vexations were ended, every shippe had gone and there were few able to save their lyves in the land of the barbarians."

It's better than I expected, thought Alec, and it's exciting too, especially that they knew how to fly. I wonder if it says anywhere in the book how they did it? It must have been part of the wisdom of Auldland, and I would like to read that, even if it's in the part that great-grandfather didn't translate.

He continued to turn the pages. Next came a passage where the strange letters were on one side and opposite them the translation. The sun! Grandpa had told him that sign stood for sun. Alec looked to see if he were right.

"The appearance of people and things is very deceptive, while their powers are not visible. We receive the light of the sun and pay no attention to it, for the light gives things their appearance and it is to this alone that we attend, although the powers of which we are not aware form the real world."

And that was a part that Alec found unreadable. He shut the book and got out of bed. Perhaps he would have another look at it, perhaps not; for the time being it went under the mattress. He looked out the window. Ah, yes, Grandpa was busy in the garden. He was walking slowly along the vegetable beds with the big watering can. The chickens were running to and fro in their coop. They wanted to get out, but they were not allowed. A chicken cannot learn to keep away from lettuce and strawberries. Alec could see the currants on the bushes. There was a pigeon sitting on the little shed.

" 'Deceptive appearances,' " said Alec. "Ha! I think the appearance is first class deluxe!"

One of the things he liked so much at Grandpa's was running into the garden in the morning, even before breakfast, and picking strawberries, a handful of currants, and a peach or an early apple, in which you could see the little drops of juice coming out when you bit into it.

"Shall I water, Grandpa?"

"Oh, no, never mind. I've nearly finished."

Alec could see that. Grandpa was watering very precisely, as if he knew exactly how thirsty a red cabbage was. And yet rain showers kept pouring down, even when the ground was already one big mud puddle. Plants knew how to deal with the water. Everything grew up again every year, and yet the weather was never exactly the same. But fruit certainly was more delicious when it ripened in the sun.

"Grandpa, do star apples turn red, even if the sun isn't shining?"

"They don't need sun, but they must have light. No life without light."

Alec nodded. He knew how nature arranged things. The entire plant was already present in the seed, however small, and what the roots got to eat mattered very little.

"Funny, really, isn't it, Grandpa? I mean: you might think that an apple tree would have red apples when it's grown on clay, green on sandy ground, and yellow if you poured on a whole lot of cow dung, but it isn't so."

"No," said Grandpa, "it isn't so." He put down the watering can. "Let me tell you something. In the house by the river we had a painting of my great-grandfather. He had narrow, pointed ears. You could see them clearly in the painting: Aulder ears. I have them, your father has them, and you have them too. And yet we all had mothers with ordinary ears. I think you are very like your mother, except for the ears."

Alec felt his ear. "So if I meet someone with ears just like ours, he may be a descendant of people who once came from Auldland too."

"That is possible. Yes. I never thought about it."

Grandpa picked up the watering can again and poured a thin stream from it every so often. Alec could hear him murmuring, "Auldland, drowned in the flood."

He's still upset about it, thought Alec, but why?

"It would be nice," said Grandpa, "if there were more of us. But they wouldn't know it themselves. They wouldn't have a book like ours. Still, they might have something else . . . something. It would be nice."

"Why, Grandpa?" asked Alec.

"Why? Then I wouldn't be alone anymore, boy. When you believe something nobody else believes, it's a poor life. They want to kill you."

"Not now, they don't. There are a whole lot of people who never go to church. You can believe what you like."

"It only seems like that. It's no longer a question of the Church. It's even fashionable to go along with all kinds of strange priests, but the earth is still the center, and for most people it's still flat! Ah . . . oh, Alec, here I stand gabbling away in my flat little garden. Come on, let's have breakfast."

Alec threw the stem of his apple into the chicken run, having already eaten the core. By now he had had two apples and at least ten strawberries, but of course they weren't real food. What he really fancied was a sandwich.

While Grandpa was still carefully spreading his own

thin slice of bread, Alec had already taken a big mouthful of a thick slice of bread and cheese. As he chewed he was thinking that he understood a little more now. Grandpa behaved so oddly about the book because he was afraid, afraid that people would think him odd because he believed what was in it.

But Alec was convinced that it didn't matter to anyone. Who would worry what an old man like that thought or believed? No one. Sometimes Alec felt wiser than Grandpa. Grandpa's time was past, and that was what made him lonely and a little sad, not the Auldland book.

"Will your friend be coming again today?" asked Grandpa.

"I don't know. We didn't arrange anything." Alec hoped very much that Chris would come. He could not imagine now what he had done here all day long before they knew each other. They were going to look at Bluebeard's chamber.

"Grandpa, is there a piece of wire in the shed?"

'Oh, yes, why?"

"For Chris's bike. Everything rattles."

"Tell him to bring his bike here. I've got screws and nuts. Wouldn't that be better?"

"Perhaps."

Alec found a not-too-badly rusted roll of wire for himself.

" 'Bye Grandpa."

Off, before Grandpa saw him. If only Chris was there! He had no wish at all to go into the castle alone.

Chris was sitting on the ground with his back to the gate, without the bike. "It collapsed under me."

"Too bad. Was Janna angry?"

"She doesn't know yet, or perhaps she does. I don't think she'll be angry. Things like bicycles don't belong in her world."

"Look, a key." Alec waved his roll of wire. "Have you ever opened a lock this way?"

"Never. Have you?"

"No, that's why I wanted to try. But if it doesn't work, I thought we could get in by the gutter from the room next door."

"I hope the murderer isn't in. Do you think murderers always sleep late? The bike is gone, in any case. I saw it lying in the woods yesterday evening. Perhaps he slept there last night."

Meanwhile, they had reached the back door. It was locked.

"That's odd. Do you think the murderer has a key? Oh, well, we'll have to go through the window again."

Alec could already feel the nervousness creeping up on him as they went in. This was no place for him. He was an intruder, and there might be a murderer in the house! He admired Chris's unconcern.

"We'll go straight upstairs," said Chris, "and if we meet anyone we'll say hello. No one knows that we are from the police and that we've been here before."

The bedroom door was wide open, and there was no one there, to Alec's relief. Up the next staircase, to the mysterious little room. They tinkered in turn with the end of the wire in the keyhole. The big roll swung in all directions. The wire had no effect at all.

"What are we going to do? The gutter?"

"Okay."

Chris was already in the next room, opening the window.

"Look out. If the thing is rusted through, we shall fall, gutter and all, and then we'll really be in a mess."

Chris put one leg through the window. "It's strong all right. Indestructible, an old thing like this."

"Wait a minute," cried Alec. "I've got a better idea. Look, there's light showing between the planks."

Under the sloping roof there were low cupboards that seemed to run through to the next room. Alec crawled inside and found he was able to see through a crack.

"Give me that wire in here."

He wriggled one end through the crack and succeeded in bringing the loop back through another split. One sharp jerk and the plank came loose.

"Have a look."

"Is there a body there? Let me see too."

"No. I don't know. A big tub."

"Pickle, of course. He has pickled the victim. What a brute! Move over now."

Chris could see the tub, but he wanted to see more. He pulled hard at the next plank, which broke with a crack. Pulling and twisting, he removed a third, and then they could slip through.

"This is called 'destruction of property.' "

"Oh, come on! Just a couple of old planks. It doesn't matter. Come and look."

There was an enormous tub in the middle of the little room, but it did not contain a pickled corpse, just the remains of some cement. It was the kind of tub masons use. There were buckets, gray boards, and proper trowels. Everything was badly rusted, and there were lumps of dried cement everywhere.

"Not pickled, bricked-in," said Chris, impressed. "So . . . our conclusion is this: the deceased is presumably still on the premises. I venture to claim, with a probability verging on certainty, that the murderer has concealed the body of his victim in this building. If only we had a dog."

"We haven't been in the cellar yet," said Alec. "Bricked-up bodies are always in cellars."

"Yes, that's true, but then it would be silly to make the cement for it up here in the attic."

"Nothing is bricked-up here, because everything is made of wood."

"All this mess doesn't really look as if it had just recently been put here. It's all very old itself."

They looked at each other indecisively. Nothing fitted anymore. Chris sat down on an upturned bucket. Alec leaned against the windowsill.

"Of course, it is possible that two offenses have been committed," said Chris, "one recently and the other, let's say, twenty years ago."

"Okay."

They said nothing more, because the affair had not grown any simpler. Chris stared thoughtfully at the gray contents of the cement tub. Alec gazed out the window. They were very high up, and he could see far over the woods. Trees, trees, a billowing sea of green.

"Chris, what is Janna to you actually?"

"Janna is a friend of the grandmother of a boy in my class."

"Oh. Nothing, in other words."

"She's a friend of mine, too, of course. I come here every vacation, because a tiny little farm in the woods is the best place I can imagine and also because Janna teaches me all kinds of things. She knows things that nobody else knows."

"What sort of things?"

"About nature. She says that all the things we see are not reality. The real world consists of powers. And she also says that it's wrong to go to school."

Alec turned. What Janna said was very like what he had read that morning, and he remembered his conversation with Grandpa in the garden.

"Do you know if Janna has narrow, pointed ears?" he asked. "Has she got ears more or less like mine?"

"She has . . ." said Chris, and then his voice stopped, because he heard something. Was there someone on the stairs? Before they had time to listen, a key was put into the lock, the door opened, and there stood a young man. The murderer?

CHAPTER VII

Murderer

"Housebreakers," said the young man. "You are thieves and housebreakers, and now I've caught you!"

Alec felt weak with fear. A murderer had caught them. They would have to overwhelm him. Did he dare to grab one of those trowels? And hit out with it? He felt weaker still.

"We're not thieves," said Chris.

"Oh, yes, you are. You ate my apples."

Chris could do nothing but laugh foolishly. He was not feeling very comfortable. The man had angry brown eyes, a thick bush of dark curls, and the beginnings of a beard. Perhaps he had just begun to let it grow, or he was only used to shaving once a week. His trousers were old and faded, and yet he did not really look like a tramp. Too clean.

"What are you doing here? Is this the headquarters of a robber band?" The young man asked.

"No, the hiding place of a murderer."

The young man whistled. "Where is the murderer and who has he murdered?"

"That's what we're finding out. We're from the police."

"Good. Then go and look somewhere else."

He made a movement with his head, and Alec and Chris obediently left the room and went down the stairs. The murderer walked calmly down behind them.

Chris believed that he was never frightened. He found it humiliating to be pushed out like this. The man was very overbearing, even though he himself was a housebreaker, if nothing worse. Halfway down the second flight, Chris had gathered his courage. Looking over his shoulder, he asked, "Have you been living here long?"

He received no answer. They reached the ground floor, and the boys moved automatically toward the back.

"How did you get in?"

"There, through the window."

They went into the garden room. The dark face now looked more thoughtful than angry. "Have you been here often?"

"Only yesterday."

"What did you find?"

"Nothing."

"Why did you say that: the hiding place of a murderer?"

"Just said it."

"Have you seen or found anything that made you think a crime has been committed here?"

"Nothing special."

Alec and Chris were beginning to get the feeling that they had been right and also that they must be very careful what they said. Alec went to the window, but the young man was ahead of him. He took a good look and found on one side a copper bolt to lock it with. He shot the bolt and said, "Go out through the back door and keep away. You may not come into the garden either. Although it has been empty for a long time, it is still private property."

He held the door open. They walked through it, and he watched them silently. Slowly Alec and Chris went out by the back door, crossed the drive, and walked up the garden path. They didn't speak to each other, but their thoughts were full of revenge. When they had reached the very end of the big garden they looked around. He was still standing there.

One at a time they nipped through the gap in the wall. At least they hadn't been murdered.

"We must warn the farmer," said Chris. "The farmer has the key to the house. He's supposed to look after it, but he probably doesn't know that the villain has moved in."

"He could simply call the police," said Alec, "but if we go there will we have to pass those dogs?"

"The dogs are harmless."

But the dogs did carry on. Chris had been in the farmyard once. He knew that they were not dangerous, but they were certainly not friendly either. "I don't think the farmer is at home now. He'll be in his fields. We'll have to go later at twelve, when everyone comes in to eat, or at half-past five."

"What I would rather find out now is what he's done."

Chris knew at once that Alec did not mean the farmer but the intruder in the castle.

"He asked so many questions, as if he himself were a detective."

"But he isn't."

"No, he's a common criminal."

They hadn't forgotten that their story about the murder was only make-believe. When they were shooting with their wooden weapons they knew perfectly well that there was no villain in the woods, and they would have had quite a shock if there had really been a pickled body in the attic room. But now they were so indignant that they wanted the young man to be a criminal.

"He asked us twice if we had found anything. There must be something hidden there."

"It might be a hundred thousand guilders. A hundred thousand guilder notes wouldn't make a very big bundle."

They were on their way to the woods. After the farm came the summer cottages. There was not much to be seen, just a few pointed roofs among the trees. There were no trailers or tents and no playground or swimming pool either. A baby was crying somewhere.

Chris was thinking about the rottentooth that Janna had talked about. It would be fun to find a hundred thousand guilders with it. But you had to know exactly what you were looking for, and Janna had not said how you were to find the rottentooth, only that it was difficult.

Chris suddenly thought of something. "Listen! Alec,

what was that you wanted to know about Janna's ears?
Just when the man surprised us, you were asking me something."

"Oh, yes," said Alec, "I was asking what they looked
like, because if she has pointed ears, she may be an Aulder
too. Grandpa would be pleased about that."

"She has thin ears. I think because she is so old. They
aren't pointed. Why should she have pointed ears? Why
should she be an Aulder?"

"Because she knows so much about powers. You said so,
didn't you? Well, the whole of that Auldland book is about
powers."

Chris gave Alec a sideways glance. "How do you know
that?"

"I saw it."

"But you don't believe in it, do you?"

"I don't, but Grandpa does. He can't talk to anyone
about it. He says that you can't just believe what you like,
and that's why he's so nervous about the book. Cracked.
And that Janna of yours is a little cracked too, isn't she?
I mean, she does all kinds of things with herbs and doesn't
talk to anyone and so on."

Chris said nothing. He wanted to think first. The woods
were very silent. They couldn't even hear their own footsteps, for the ground was soft and springy. Just now and
then a dry twig would crack: *tick*.

Alec was looking sideways. Could Chris be angry? "Don't
you like me saying that about Janna?"

"You're quite right. She's as mad as a hatter." Chris

laughed aloud. "But it wouldn't do your grandpa any good if her knowledge did come from Auldland, and that may well be true. She never talks about it. I just know she can't stand men or books either. Everything she knows is so secret that it's never been written down; she learned it from her mother and grandmother. Passed on. Exactly the way your book is passed on from fathers to sons."

"Has Janna got a daughter?"

"No, she's got me. And she doesn't like it at all that I'm a boy." Chris laughed again, but he said no more.

Alec began to have a creepy feeling: this mystery again. Surely Chris had said that she was not part of his family? A friend of his grandmother, or of a friend's grandmother, something like that. So why should she be teaching him those things about nature? Funny business. Walking discontentedly over the mossy ground, he was beginning to think, What are we doing here, why am I going along with Chris?

Then Chris stood still, one hand raised. Listen. That was not a single dry twig, that was the snapping and cracking of masses of dead wood. Someone was trying to find a way between the trees, stamping with a pair of feet . . . that might well be size thirteen.

At once the boys were back in their game, half game, half revenge. Of course, their villain must be the one who was thrusting the bushes aside with his long arms to make a path for himself. They had plenty of time to hide, for he was not approaching the path in their direction. In fact, it sounded as if he were finding the very thickest undergrowth deliberately. He had a knife with which he was hacking off tiresome branches. They could not see if he was doing anything else besides destroying plants, but that was bad enough. Suddenly he turned sharply, and Alec and Chris dived deep into the bracken. Now he *was* coming in their direction. They could make out that he was zigzagging wildly. He seemed to be looking for something.

"He has lost his hundred thousand guilders," whispered Chris.

"We really ought to keep ahead of him. Then we will find them."

"Unbelievably stupid, a thief who loses his spoils."

"I think he's found them now. He's standing still."

Then they heard a different kind of crack. The young man had taken a vicious kick at something made of metal. Chris straightened up. He had a suspicion of what it might be. And then he saw that he was right and flew headlong into the attack.

"My bike! Vandal! First making big holes in this beautiful wood, and then kicking someone else's perfectly good things to bits! What do you think you're doing?"

Without taking any notice of the big knife that the man was still holding and that Alec was regarding with horror, he stooped to pick up the damaged vehicle.

"Busted. Look at it! Unusable. And how am I to get home now?"

"Sorry," said the villain, "I'm really sorry. You can have mine."

CHAPTER VIII

Yellow Bicycle

The young man threw his knife to the ground and plumped down in the midst of the long-stemmed forest plants that poked up in the shadows between dry twigs and leaves. The part of his face that was not covered with black stubble looked sweaty and dirt-streaked. He wiped it with the sleeve of his shirt, adding a brown streak beside his nose. Then he combed his fingers through his mop of hair.

"I thought it was an abandoned bike, it looks so old, and I felt like kicking something. Mine is down at the farm. It's yellow. If you don't mind passing the dogs, you can have it."

Chris could not take in what he was saying. Suddenly the man did not seem villainous at all. Of course, this was the moment to be careful.

"Does the farmer know you're here?"

"Of course. When I'm not here he keeps an eye on the

house. That has always been the arrangement." Once again there was anger in the dark face. Then he stood up.

"I'll come down to the farm with you. Otherwise, he may well think you are thieves." A snort of laughter.

"The bike was very old," said Chris, "and a little broken too. I don't need another one."

"Come with me."

He strode off, the dangerous knife hanging in his hand. A few brown leaves had stuck to his jeans. And the boys followed him.

On the way Alec suddenly gave a spurt of nervous laughter. He was imagining how it would look to see an old woman with a pipe on a bright-yellow man's bike.

Chris was thinking, We shouldn't believe him, but I want to know everything about him and that's why I'm going with him. "Were you looking for something in the woods, sir?"

"Yes."

They had reached the farm. He opened the gate, and the dogs began to sniff, growling, at the boys. Alec was terrified, but he decided not to show it. They could see the yellow bicycle leaning against the barn.

"Slot!" shouted the villain, with all the masterfulness you could get into such a small word. "Slot!"

The door of the house opened. First the scent of roast ham drifted out. Then a short, broad man in clogs came hurrying awkwardly and stiffly forward. "Yes, sir?"

"Slot, these boys are to have my bike. But remember, they're not allowed into the garden or the house."

"Right, sir."

"There you are, take it."

"Thank you," said Chris, "but you can keep it. I think I'll just have the other one fixed up."

Then they made off from the farmyard at full speed, and this time they did not go into the woods but back to the road.

"He acts as if he were everybody's boss, but in my opinion he's a housebreaker."

"Mine too. He says that the castle is his and the farmer believes him, but I don't believe a word of it."

"Some farmers are terribly stupid."

"Grandpa says there has never been anyone in the castle as long as he's lived here, and that's fifteen years."

"Janna says it's been empty more than twenty years. And after all, this fellow is under thirty."

"Just a nasty housebreaker."

"Of course, that's why he wanted to give me the bicycle. He thought he could keep us quiet with it. But I don't need his silly old yellow bike."

"It's too bad, really. It's a good one. But you were terrific. 'I'll have the other one fixed up!' Ha, ha, that old piece of iron! You'll come for lunch again, won't you? What time is it?"

"Quarter-past twelve."

Only then did Alec realize that Chris did not wear a watch. "How did you know?"

"I guessed. It might be five minutes earlier or later, but it won't be more than that."

"Did you guess because the farmer was already having his lunch?"

"That too. It's one of the things I learned from Janna. You think of nothing for a moment, and then you just know. First you often guess wrong, and suddenly you can do it. I can wake up when I want to in the mornings too."

Alec could scarcely believe him.

There was Grandpa's cottage, the little front garden with the begonias and the periwinkles. Open the gate, shut the gate, *tonk*.

"Oh, hey, Chris, I've just remembered. Listen, you mustn't ask for the book, understand? Don't talk about the book at all today, please."

"Why not?"

"Because . . . I'll tell you later. Hi, Grandpa, here's Chris again. Is that okay?"

"Of course, of course. It will work out very well. I happen to have picked at least a pound of strawberries. They need eating."

Alec was still afraid that Chris might start talking to Grandpa about the Auldland book. Then Grandpa would take it out of the cupboard and notice that the other one was not there. Alec had no idea yet how he was going to put it back again, but that could come later. He began to talk about the castle. Who did it really belong to? What had Grandpa heard about it during the years he had lived here?

There was little enough Grandpa could tell them. The days when there had been feasting and hunting in the woods were long past. The last inhabitant had been a man of about fifty who lived there as a recluse and had finally been taken away.

"He didn't think like other people," said Grandpa, "so he had to go to the madhouse. If you don't think like everyone else, it's better not to talk about it."

"Did he talk about it? What did he think?" asked Alec curiously.

"I don't know, boy. I don't know anything about it. It's all so long ago."

He probably thought that strawberries and plates and tables didn't exist, that only powers exist, thought Alec. But aloud he said, "And then?"

"Then for the first few years it stayed as it was," said Grandpa. "Later they took the furniture out, but the house was never sold. No one ever came to look at it again, and it wasn't kept up, nor were the woods, of course. For years no one was allowed to set foot in them, but that was gradually forgotten. You can walk there, but only along the edge. If you go any farther, the growth becomes impenetrable. There are no more paths and no firebreaks. It's a shame, because there are some fine old trees. I think they get stifled when the undergrowth isn't cut away. Perhaps they will make a road through there someday. The villages on the other side are eight miles away, and if you could go straight through it would be about four."

"I expect there are poachers," said Chris.

"Very probably."

"Does Janna live at the edge of the woods?" asked Alec. "How far is it to walk?"

"A long way. It's a pity I haven't got a bike now."

"Wasn't the wire any good?" asked Grandpa.

"It's completely wrecked," said Chris. "Nothing can be done about it now."

Oh Lord, thought Alec, Grandpa noticed that I took that old roll of wire, and I can't even give it back, because it's still in Bluebeard's chamber.

Would he be annoyed about it? He might. He was fussy about the most trivial things. "It's because of the war," Grandpa always said. "Since we lost everything in the war, I can't throw anything away." Well, that was a long time ago. Grandpa didn't really fit in anymore. As Alec was thinking that, he suddenly felt very warmly toward Grandpa. He must say something nice.

"Any shopping you want done, Grandpa?"

"Tomorrow will do."

"I'll do it right away. It's as good as done."

On the window seat there was a piece of paper on which Grandpa had written in pencil: one package cornstarch, black shoe polish, one pound coffee, four pounds sugar.

"Okay," said Alec, "all from Slot, I suppose?"

The shopkeeper in the village was called Slot, like the farmer by the castle. Grandpa took a little pencil out of a drawer and added another item: a package of peppermints.

"All from Slot, and you can keep the peppermints."

"Could they be licorice? I like those better."

They could. They were given as much money as they needed. Alec looked back once more. He was going off with Chris again, and Grandpa would have to wash the dishes alone. Tomorrow he would stay at home for once.

* * *

"Now what was that about the book? Why wasn't I allowed to mention it?"

"Oh, yes." Reluctantly Alec told him about the other book, in which his great-great-great-grandfather had rewritten the story of his great-great-great-great- (and at least another twenty greats) grandfather, and he also told Chris where it was now.

Chris was quite uncontrollable afterward. He walked twice as fast in order to get back all the sooner. "And then I shall say, 'Alec, can I see your bedroom?' And then we'll hide the book under our shirts, and we'll go—"

"No," said Alec.

"Why not? We won't hurt it. I don't even need to touch it. You can hold on to it yourself. You can read it out. I only want to know what's in it."

"I'm not going to take it out of the house."

"Then we'll look at it there. Only there is the risk that your grandpa might come upstairs. Perhaps we would be able to hide it in time."

Alec thought about the inexplicably exaggerated care with which Grandpa treated the book. He could not go off and look at it with a friend, just like that. "I don't want to. I shall look at it again tonight or tomorrow morning. I'll tell you everything I read."

"Tell me what you've already read."

" 'Gone for my life's sake to kirk.' Funny, isn't it? Alec Auldland went to the church to save his life. Oh, yes, and it says that the Aulders could fly and that almost all of them were drowned and . . . well, after that it was about powers and appearances. I didn't really understand it. It was very boring to read."

"Oooh!" Chris groaned. "Why are you an Aulder and not I? I suppose you wouldn't like to learn to fly?"

"And I suppose you think you could learn to from that old book?"

Chris thought he could. He had reason to believe it. In his short life he had already known many things that should not have been possible and yet had happened.

The strange things had begun when he had found a beautiful stone. After a while he had noticed that he had a special contact with someone he was thinking of if he held the stone firmly. He suddenly knew things the other person knew but had not said aloud, and he could even make someone think or do things.

If he wanted to, he could make Alec turn back now, even before he had done the shopping. Alec would take the book out from under the mattress and say, "Here you are. You look at it in peace. I know I'll get it back from you sometime." Alec himself would think it was his own idea, but of course later on he would regret it.

And that was why Chris was not allowed to use the stone. As soon as he had it, he met other people who practiced supernatural arts. There was an association, with rules and duties. Chris was not entirely in agreement with it. He did not even know for sure if he wanted to belong to the association, but the fact that he could not put a spell on someone just as he liked seemed to him a reasonable rule. Chris was not even allowed to use the stone for a whole year. They had explained to him that only this way could he learn to remain master of himself.

Now he went about with the stone in a matchbox in his pocket, and he was not allowed to touch it. When he had promised he had not thought it was going to be so difficult. However, everything, everything connected with the stone was difficult. He was here with Janna in order to learn the secrets of the craft from her. Janna was very good and he had been glad, but it was no fun. Learning witchcraft was far more difficult than the things he learned at school, and on the whole it didn't get you anywhere either. How hard he had had to work, learning to feel the time! It was more trouble than looking at the clock, and if he wore a watch for only a few days, his efforts became less successful right away.

And another tiresome thing was that you could never talk about it. People always began to laugh in a particular way when anything about the supernatural came up. Alec was the same. Chris knew quite well that Alec was thinking he was cracked when he had said something about flying. A hopeless case, that Alec.

Deep inside, Chris was complaining—as he turned the little box in his pocket over and over again.

There was the shop. They had to carry a metal basket over one arm. There was no room for carts, and there was only one cashier. Fat Mrs. Slot sat behind it. Everything went rather slowly, because she was so scared of making mistakes that she added everything up twice over on a scrap of paper and also had to explain why she was doing so.

Alec had collected what he needed in a moment, and there they stood. There was an old woman in front of them. She had all Mrs. Slot's attention. When the boys heard what she was talking about, she had their attention too.

"What do you think, Miss Roterdink? Did he really inherit the castle? He rides around on a yellow bicycle."

"It seems to be quite true. He looks exactly like the old gentleman, and he looks at you in the same way."

"But his name is not Hazelhurst."

"He must be a son of Miss Jaqueline. The other one never had any children, and neither did the old gentleman, of course."

"You must know, you worked there for years. But I think it's funny all the same. One of the gentlemen from the castle, on a yellow bicycle. They were so terribly rich."

CHAPTER IX

Prophecy

Alec and Chris were out of doors again. Each had a
mouthful of licorice. Miss Roterdink was walking ahead
of them with her black-striped shopping bag. The weather
was hot and sunny, but she was still wearing a coat, a thin
black one with a small fur collar.

Grandpa lived outside the village. First they had to
pass two meadows and afterward came a row of six iden-
tical cottages. The last was Grandpa's, and outside the
first, as they could see from a distance, stood the yellow
bicycle. Someone had called. He was just about the same
height as the front door, beside which he stood watching,
his hands behind his back. Miss Roterdink had begun to
walk a little faster, but still the boys had almost overtaken
her when she opened the gate and nervously searched for
her key in the depths of her bag. The door closed behind
the two of them as Chris and Alec reached the gate.
B. Roterdink, they saw painted on the gate in slanting
letters.

"She ought to watch out who she takes into her house," said Alec.

However, Chris said, "I think perhaps we had better think up a different game now."

"You're probably right."

By now neither of them really believed in their murderer any longer. Slot the farmer, Slot the shopkeeper, and Miss Roterdink might all be wrong, but the man would not voluntarily go to see someone who knew the Hazelhurst family well if he was anyone other than he claimed to be.

"Coming with me, Chris?"

"No, I'll keep on going. It's so far."

"Here, for the walk."

Alec shook one or two licorice candies into his own hand and passed over the rest of the package to Chris.

" 'Bye."

"Same to you."

Alec went in through the back door. The whole of the little kitchen was filled with steam, the lid was dancing on the kettle, and Grandpa was standing looking out, with a teaspoon in his hand.

"Grandpa, are you all right?"

"No," said Grandpa. "I mean yes." With a sigh he put some tea in the teapot and then a little bit more. Only then did he take the rattling kettle off the stove and fill the pot. He put the hot kettle down on the tablecloth.

Oh, Lord, thought Alec, he must have missed the book. Now it's coming.

At home there would have been no problem. To his

father or mother, he would have said, "You said yourself
that I could have it," or, "Don't make such a fuss, nothing
has happened to it." But Grandpa was different. He took
things so hard.

"Alec, did you see where I left the little book? It's not
in the box."

"You didn't put it in the box, Grandpa. I know just
where it is. Shall I get it?"

"Oh," said Grandpa, "what luck! I was beginning to be
afraid I was so old I had started to forget things."

Alec was up the stairs and down again in three jumps.

"Here it is, Grandpa."

"Thank you. What luck! I wanted to look something
up, and it was gone."

"I wanted to look something up too. That's why I took
it upstairs with me when you forgot to hide it away."

Ha, ha, thought Alec, that wasn't too bad. Not until he
had finished his tea and saw Grandpa's shock at the pitch-
black ring on the white tablecloth did he think, Grandpa
is so old that he forgets things. He forgot to pack up the
book, and he put the kettle in the wrong place. But he
doesn't know it himself.

"Now tell me what you wanted to look up."

"About the cooked friend. Oh, yes, and about the
prophecy, too."

"Let's have a look."

Grandpa went to find his glasses. He opened the book
and immediately found the right place. He read it aloud,
pointing with one finger.

" 'To find this friend, you must first be freshly washed

and light of heart. Then should you walk under fruit-bearing trees, which are full sound and have not the smallest rot or taint and are continually in the light of the sun, such that its light reaches to their roots. Taking care not to tread upon these roots, it may be that you will find small gray threads upon them, which swiftly disappear when moist. Having cleaned this friend, you shall prepare it in a glazed earthenware pan with a little rainwater and leave it to boil merrilie on a coal fire and strain it through hair sieve or clean cloth. He who drinks this liquid in sobriety shall be enabled to find any thinge that is lost.' "

"Oh," said Alec.

"Yes," said Grandpa, "that's what it says. I think there is more about it in the real book. The beginning has gone, or there is a sentence missing after the bit about the gray threads. But it clearly says that the friend has to be cooked. Perhaps it is a kind of bird. In the old days they used to eat thrushes and larks. It may well be that there was a bird known as friend."

Alec's interest was no longer very strong, but he had promised Chris that he would read the book and tell him something about it. He must take care to remember this strange description. So you had to walk under a fruit tree and not tread on the roots.

"Have you ever tried it, Grandpa?"

"Tried what?"

"To see if there are threads growing under the apple tree."

No, Grandpa had never thought of that. He had read and reread the puzzling translation of his precious legacy. For years he had done his best to understand some part of it, because he believed what was written there was true. But it was still just a book, something outside the course of daily life.

"And what was the other thing you wanted to know? The prophecy that the house would burn down?"

"Oh, was that in there? Did that very old book say that the house on the river would go up in flames?"

"Not exactly. Just that on that particular night the book must be taken out of the house. I told you that, didn't I?"

"Yes," said Alec, "but I didn't quite understand." Suddenly he realized why it was a prophecy. "The book had to be out of the house, not the people? They could burn to death, I suppose. How mean!"

"Perhaps we would have gone away too, if we could have read it for ourselves. The translation is very complicated. I'll look it up again."

"No, Grandpa, don't do that. I would rather read this bit over again, and then I can tell Chris about it. He wants to know all about it. Or isn't that allowed?"

"Chris had better come again if he is so keen, and then he can see for himself."

"But I thought you didn't want anyone to touch it! You said the book must not go out of the house, and you always put it back in the cupboard before I've had a good look at it."

"Someone with a feeling for it may always look at it. But not if it's just for the language or the letters. I cannot allow people to laugh at it, Alec, or to be unbelieving. When I feel that you're thinking, silly old Grandpa with his book, I hide it deep in the cupboard. And in my experience almost everyone does think like that. But Chris doesn't. I would let him look at the book. Just you tell him that."

"Okay," said Alec, "I will." But he was not quite sure if he was really glad about it.

Chris had walked the long way home to Janna's house in the woods. There were tall, ancient oaks around it, and the sun shone aslant on the thatched roof. There was a golden haze over the yard. Little sounds bubbled up everywhere, and familiar things moved softly: a mouse, a kitten, a row of fat pigeons on the dovecote, hens pecking, geese scratching, and the short, angry hiss of Janna's broom outside the low green door. The setting was as quiet and peaceful as if time did not exist, although it was obviously late afternoon.

Chris stood still, looking around.

"Kraaa!" shrieked the crow on the edge of the well, and Janna looked up.

"So there you are. You can find Janna's house when you're hungry, can you?"

"Always," said Chris. "You know that, Janna. Your house goes on calling, even when I'm not hungry."

Chris knew that Janna had felt he was on his way half

an hour ago and that she was sweeping so industriously now to show him how busy she was. Chris was not at all impressed. "Janna, can you fly with that broom?" he asked.

She stopped sweeping and gave him a sideways glance. "Why do you want to know? Are you supposed to tell the heads of the association what Janna is up to? Do they want me out of it again because I do the forbidden things: flying, moving dead things, turning live things to stone? Rules, rules, rules, bah! I don't need the association anymore. What's the use of an art if you do nothing with it? Tell me that."

"I'm not saying anything. I've got nothing to do with the association. I just wanted to know if it's really possible to fly on a broomstick, like the fairy tales. It says in Alec's book that the Aulders could fly, and I would love to learn. It would be better than feeling the time, when there are so many clocks around."

"Of course it's possible. You learn it for yourself. You just have to release your weight from the places where the earth is pulling. But it's no good thinking that flying is more fun or easier than feeling the time. You might just as well go bicycling. Where is the bicycle?"

"Busted."

"Oh. Well, it was high time. I had it when I was twenty-five. Got it from the baron. Hee-hee-hee-hee-hee." Janna laughed her bleating laugh and stood the broom against the wall. As she went indoors Chris could hear her muttering under her breath, "Flying. As if that was anything special. Anyone can learn. They just think they can't do it. Once upon a time they thought bicycling was impossible, keeping your balance on two thin wheels. And now everyone does it, hee-hee-hee-hee."

She put the black kettle on the fire and began to cut the heavy, homemade bread. Chris took the bowl with the honeycomb from Janna's own bees and the pot with the butter in it from the cow called Bessie. As he reached for the elder-blossom tea, Janna banged the knife down on the table with great force, and he jumped.

"But you can't learn it from a book," she began to scold, "and now I'm going to tell you exactly what the trouble is with books. I know, because once upon a time I read one right through to the end. When you read, you break away from the earth and you become as dry as paper. You don't notice it in the town, of course, where a stony crust stifles the land, but you notice it on the open ground, which is growing and breathing. Here. When you are here you can feel nature, because you are part of it. You know when the rain is coming, you listen to the trees, and you can smell what time of year it is."

Janna looked at Chris impatiently to make sure he was listening. "Yes, and then you read a book. All kinds of things are written in it and at best it is good, but the feeling in it comes from another person in another time and another place. And for you it's all wrong. Then when you hear a bird twitter, you don't even know why. It may be calling its mate or feeding its young. You don't know, because your head is full of the stale life of someone you never met. Your thoughts get muddled, because the words are broken up into letters and the power has gone out of them. That's what books do: take away power. Isn't that bad?"

"Yes," said Chris. He had heard it all before and knew quite well what she meant. He had better not let her hear any more talk about Alec and the Auldland book.

Janna grew calmer, began to cut more bread, and stopped again. There was enough already. From the fire she took a circular pan, whose contents went on bubbling when it was on the table. It was full of black toadstools that rose and sank again in a thick brown soup.

"Are those rottentooth fungus?"

"Not at all. Do you need some? Have you lost something?"

"I haven't. Someone else has." And Chris told her about the young man in the castle who was searching for something.

"At first we thought he was a villain, but he really is a member of the family who used to live here."

"A young Hazelhurst!" said Janna. "You don't have to help him. Let him go on looking alone. If he intends to turn the whole house and the woods upside down, he'll have his work cut out."

"I wasn't thinking of helping him," said Chris, "but it would be fun to find what he's looking for."

Janna narrowed her fierce eyes until they were almost closed. "Yes," she said, "that really might be fun."

CHAPTER X

Questions

Miss Roterdink set out coffee. Luckily she had just baked fresh cookies. There had only been four left in the tin, and that would have looked inhospitable. She was not sure what to do with her unexpected guest. He was very like the last inhabitant of Hazelhurst Castle, where she had worked so long, but *he* had always been a respectable gentleman, however strangely he had begun to behave in the end. This young man did not look like a gentleman, in his shabby trousers and sloppily rolled-up sleeves. And his name was Vandyck. Miss Jaqueline could surely have done better than that! In Miss Roterdink's mind the population of the Netherlands consisted of a whole stair-case of classes, and you simply must not marry someone more than one or two steps away from your own class. That was why she herself had never married. After the long years at the castle she did not fit in anywhere.

The young William Vandyck was having just as much

difficulty with her. He lacked the good-natured friendliness of his Uncle William, and if he was even a little bit embarrassed he looked very cross. He had visited the castle once, at the age of five, when it had a whole staff of servants to look after one old gentleman who was growing madder every day. He thought that was an offensive and unjust state of affairs, and he believed that the staff thought so too, but this old maid didn't. She acted humbly, yet at the same time she showed that she disapproved of him. But she must help him!

"Do you understand my problem?" He was beginning to talk quite formally. "The house will have to be sold and probably the woods as well, although we know that there must be money hidden somewhere, a lot of money, and other valuables too. I was hoping that you might have seen something. You were there night and day, weren't you?"

"Certainly, but the baron would not have told me where he hid his possessions."

"Of course I could part with some of it. It would be worth really a lot to me if it were found and that was why I hoped you might have some idea where the money has gone. There is cement at the top of the house. If anything in the house had been bricked up, there would have been a damp patch and dirty footprints at the time. You would know about that."

"Nowhere except upstairs. Would you care for another cookie, Mr. Vandyck? Can I pour you some more coffee?"

"No, thank you. Have you really seen nothing?"

"No." She shook her head and blew her nose. She had nothing to tell him.

"Did he give things away? The gold tobacco box? I saw that myself when I was small. He kept tobacco in it that was grown by the gardener—big leaves."

"He did give a few things away—the baron was always generous—but not the gold tobacco box with the family coat-of-arms, of course."

Miss Roterdink had once been given a crystal bowl and a little silver vase, but he did not need to know that.

He went on questioning, "What did my uncle do all day long? Did he ever go to see people in the village?" And "To whom did he talk most?"

She shrugged her thin shoulders. "If I knew where he had hidden the money I would tell you, honestly, but I never saw any of these things, and if Slot knows nothing, I know nothing either."

There, she could go no farther. She put the lid on the cookie tin, and William Vandyck stood up. He thanked her for her patience and left. She watched him through the draped curtains. Would he be thinking over that last sentence? She could not tell this boy about that thing, could she? Nobody knew that she had seen it. It surely had nothing to do with valuables. She sighed deeply. The conversation had thoroughly upset her. All the foolishness of the past had come to the surface again. Poor old man! No one in the family had done anything when he had been so unhappy, and now they wanted his money. Why now and not before? Oh, well, it did not signify. They need not come to her again. She already regretted having uttered that one sentence. The unexpectedness of the visit had shocked her into it. But she would never again tell anyone what she knew. The old gentleman was dead; the Hazelhurst family was over and done with. It was all in the past. She went to wash up the cups, her eyes filled with tears.

William Vandyck pedaled to his castle on his yellow bicycle and climbed the bare wooden stairs. Slumping into a deckchair, he said, "Wishy-washy coffee."

Then he drank half a bottle of beer at one draft. He had a paper with marks on it. It was a list of the places where he had searched and the people who might know something. He could put a line through Miss Roterdink. What had come of it?

Then he began to think the conversation over. "If Slot knows nothing, I know nothing either." The bottle of beer was emptied. So Slot did know something! But he had questioned him so often. What was the best way of getting that wooden man to talk? If only he had something of the presence of an old-time lord of the manor. People still looked up to that role here obviously. But he could not suddenly put on a white shirt and a necktie and begin all over again, could he? Then he would have to start shaving again too. He scratched at his stubbly beard. It was just beginning to look quite real.

First he would have a bite to eat, and then back to see Slot. The bread was dry, like a piece of wood. The peanut butter was like putty. "Just wait," William told himself, "in a while I'll be rich. Then I'll eat smoked salmon and steak and meringue pudding every day." He thought sadly of his mother's meringue pudding. She used to put eight eggs in it, he remembered that. Miss Roterdink had taught her. His mother had been able to get along very well with the people here. She had been dead a long time now.

Slot was just riding into the farmyard on the tractor. He saw the tall young man and thought, There he is again. His face showed nothing. He drove the tractor to its place and came trotting up, apparently making great haste, but he took a long time, all the same, to cross that little bit of yard. William was not aware of it.

"Ah, Slot," said William. Once again he sounded much too abrupt. He cleared his throat.

"Yes, sir, good day, sir," said Slot.

"I wanted to ask another question. I've just been with Miss Roterdink. It seems to me it would be best to tell me honestly how things stand, Slot."

"Yes, sir."

"She said something, which I have been thinking over. She said, 'If Slot knows nothing, I know nothing either.' And now it seems to me that the position is this: there must be something to tell. And I can imagine that my uncle swore you to silence, and I can also understand that you prefer to say nothing."

"Yes, sir."

Oh, damn, thought William, it's all going wrong again.

I'm just standing here stammering. Why is it that I can't talk to the man? Why does he shut me out? He never asks me in.

"Slot?"

"Yes, sir."

"Please, man, do help me! What is the point of behaving so secretively?"

"Yes, sir. It's like this, sir. My lord baron was a bit confused in his later years. You know about that. There would be a whole lot to tell, but it would do no good to the memory of my lord baron, nor to you, sir. It's no good to anyone, dragging those things up again. You must just think: perhaps it is all gone. Perhaps my lord baron sold the jewels and spent all the money. You might as well stop searching, sir."

"Miss Roterdink thinks you know something."

"Well, it's like this, sir. Perhaps she meant my father. In those days my father went to the castle more than I did. He went through a great many things with my lord baron. My father and old Rengerink."

"Rengerink? I don't know him."

"Jan Rengerink, he was the gardener."

"But he's dead."

"Yes, he is, sir. He was born in 1880, like my father. There's not many left alive from those days."

William got the feeling that Slot was making a fool of him. There was an invisible wall through which he could not pass. "Thank you then, Slot, and good-bye."

"Yes, sir, good-bye sir."

William trudged back through the garden, past the moss-covered greenhouse, the rose garden where a few heavy roses hung their heads. Slot had pruned them regularly. Everything else had gone wild, but it was warm and peaceful in the late sun. He sat on the steps by the kitchen door and looked at his neglected property.

"Am I to believe these people and accept that there is nothing?" he asked himself. "Sell the whole thing and go away? And then read in the newspapers in a year or two that treasure has been found on the former Hazelhurst estate?" He shook his head. Slot had not convinced him, nor had Miss Roterdink. What were they hiding from him, and why?

In his room in Leiden there was a note he had found in his Aunt Reine's desk. He had read it so often that he knew the contents by heart.

"To my nephew, William Vandyck.

"When, after my death, you come into possession of our ancestral estate, I advise you not to sell the house at once, because in it, or close to it, there will probably be your Uncle William's coin collection.

"On my visits to him over the years he spent in the Happyhill Institution, he repeatedly made references to the sensible way, in his eyes, in which he had hidden this valuable possession. However, he never told me exactly where, since he always thought he was being spied on. In any case, conversations with him were made very unpleasant by the indecent remarks he was always making.

"On his death I had intended to travel down to look

after this and that, but the memory of disagreeable situa-
tions held me back for a while. I did not need the money
luckily, but it must not fall into the wrong hands.

"It will be best to get in touch with Jan, the gardener.
The Slot family is also to be trusted."

William had been surprised when he found the note. He
had visited his Aunt Reine every month. Why had she not
told him about it? She must have had certain suspicions.
And he could have gone to look years ago, if she had not
wanted to herself. A valuable coin collection! It was
ridiculous just to leave it there, however sensibly hidden
it was.

He had gone over all the old memories connected with
Uncle William and Hazelhurst Castle. At home they were
always quite mysterious about the mad uncle who shamed
them. But he had picked up one or two things. Aunt Reine,
coming to his mother in a terrible state, had said, "Now
William has sold another two farms!" And, "William has
gone to an auction sale in London to buy antique coins in
a track suit! Jaqueline, a track suit!"

Had the two things happened at the same time? Had
Uncle William bought coins to the value of two farms?
That was quite something, and then there must be a
jeweled cross, as well, and things like the tobacco box.

William stood up, brushed the dust off his jeans, and
stamped the sand off his big shoes. He still did not intend
to give up, but all the same he had little hope. Had Uncle
William really never told anyone anything? Who had been
involved when he was finally taken away? A doctor, nurses.

Who had been in the house all those years, unnoticed, like the two boys, or doing a job, like moving men and painters? Not much had been done to the house, but something had. And where else could he look? He had searched everywhere. Despondently he started on his last bottle of beer.

CHAPTER XI

Janna

The black fungus soup was finished, and Janna packed Chris off to look for eggs. She herself sat on quietly at the table. She had opened the oven door, and the red glow lighted her face. A glittering flame seemed to burn in each of her small, dark eyes. Janna was thinking over what she had just heard: a young Hazelhurst was patrolling the castle in search of something. It would be fun if Chris found it certainly, but Janna had a better idea. It would be much nicer if she herself succeeded in taking what the young man wanted so much.

When she had stared into the flames for some time, Janna decided that this was what must happen. She would see to it. Not today, tomorrow. The boy, Chris, would have to look after the house. She would think up some little job for him, and she would also have to decide what she herself was supposed to be doing, because no one must know the truth.

At this point Chris returned with the eggs. "Back already? I'm sure you didn't look behind the pigsty. The brown hen with the little tuft has a nest behind the pigsty. Go and have a look."

Christ went off again obediently. Janna poked a couple of faggots through the stove door. They began to burn at once, crackling. Gazing with satisfaction as they were rapidly consumed, she muttered softly to herself.

Tomorrow she would really get to work again. She felt like it. Of course, even Janna could not know what the young man was actually looking for. Still less had she any idea where she might find it. But that did not trouble her in the least. She had a strong suspicion who had hidden it, which was enough for her. Janna had known William, Baron Hazelhurst, very well indeed.

Next morning she rose early, and when Chris came out to wash at the well, he saw a pair of small clogs with pointed toes drying out. Janna had whitened them with a chalk-and-water paste. She tied a blue apron over her black skirt and a woolen shawl over a white-dotted jacket. Chris had never seen her look this way before.

"Janna, is there going to be a party? Is it your birthday?"

She shook her head. Her hair had been tugged back into a stiff knot, full of hairpins.

"A bird came here last night," said Janna, "with a message. Somebody needs me. An old friend is sick, and I shall have to walk through the wood and stand by the roadside. When the bus comes along, I shall put out my hand. Then I have to sit in the bus for an hour, and half an hour after that. I must get out and walk for another quarter of an hour. On the bend in the road stands a house. It has a red roof, a green door, and a little blue curtain at the window. The key is behind a flowerpot. I am to go in and put on the kettle. The leaf of a giant hogweed must be ground fine, together with the leaf of a royal fern. That drives the evil vapors away. Then I shall cook a tea of thyme and watermint to make good vapors, and my old friend will come back again."

"Where's he now? Who is it?"

"You don't know him. He's in his own bed in the house with the red roof. By 'come back' I mean that he will get better again. When someone is sick, he creeps away inside himself, where time and place have no meaning. Look, I have everything with me. I just have to look for the giant hogweed on the way. It doesn't grow hereabouts. You have to put yourself out for people."

She looked straight at Chris. He knew that she was thinking, You *must* believe me. Therefore, he did not believe her. Janna could not get used to the fact that he was already advanced in the magical arts. She could not deceive him.

"And I?" he asked. "What do I do?"

"You must take Bessie to the fields today. You must put the apples in the attic and feed the cats and the hens. You must pick beans and peel potatoes, and if you have time you can sweep the threshing floor."

"Okay," said Chris. If Janna wanted to do something on her own for once, he was quite willing.

"When the sun is over the roof of the barn, you have your bread and cheese and the stewed pears from yesterday, and when the sun has passed the dovecote, you can put on the potatoes, because I shall already have left the bus. And when I have passed the big white birch, William the crow will come and call from the well so you can put out the dishes, because I shall be very busy when I get home."

"Okay," said Chris, "have a good trip. I'll do everything you said." And he thought to himself, Perhaps this is the first time in Janna's whole life that she has gone out for a day and someone has taken care of everything for her here.

Janna stepped into the white clogs. She pushed all the plants deep down into her basket and set out. A few yards behind her trotted the black cat, followed by the orange tom and a young black kitten. Three, no four, five big crows flew calmly from tree to tree in the same direction. She did not turn her head once. When Chris could no longer see her, he went indoors. First he would clear up and then see to the cow.

Janna walked silently over the coarse grass and moss, her skirts trailing. When she was deep enough among the trees she sent the cats home again. "Be off, I don't need you." And soon afterward she sent the crows as well. "Go on, William, you must keep watch."

She sighed deeply once and looked about her. Come, just a little farther. The trees were tall and dense; very little sunlight penetrated them and there was no wind at all. She did not need the shawl. She folded it in half and

then again, smaller and smaller, into a wad. Finally she
slipped off her clogs and pulled all the hairpins out of the
hard little bun behind her head. She even unraveled the
thin braid that was left. The clogs, the shawl, everything
went into the basket, including the black knitted stockings.

"That's how it was," said Janna softly.

She was no longer used to walking barefoot, but it felt
wonderful. She shook her hair loose and tried to feel young
again. A tough old woman, she was longing to be the merry,
lively girl she had once been. There was no one in the
wood to see her. Yes, there was someone. Janna froze and
listened. Had she heard something? She felt as if someone
were watching her, the feeling you get when you think you
are alone in a room and suddenly you know that there is
someone else there. It lasted for a moment. Then Janna
knew who it was—a fox. She could not see it, she could hear
nothing, but she knew. A fox was somewhere close by,
staring alertly at her. Perhaps it had cubs. Janna picked up
the basket and walked on. Chris hadn't anything to do
with what she was up to, nor did the cats, nor did that fox.
She was deeper in the woods now, far from the path that
Chris often took. She saw the blue wings of a jay flapping,
and two inquisitive squirrels saw her. She came to a brown
beech tree and a huge acacia.

"It was here," said Janna softly.

She set the basket down carelessly and wandered around,
rather less cheerful now, no longer caring whether squirrels or anyone else were looking on. She was more like a
young girl than she had been a few minutes before. Janna

sat down with her back to the acacia. There were masses of bilberries. She sniffed. The smell of bilberries was everywhere, but different in every place.

"This was the place," said Janna softly.

She sat there for a long time, recalling the past. She could see him again, the baron in his fine riding boots. The very first time they had met by the acacia she had known that she could cast a spell over him with her nimble, butter-fly ways.

"Janna, you fly, you never touch the grass."

"Janna, stay a moment. Janna, listen."

"Janna . . . Janna . . . Janna. . . ."

By the acacia tree, under orange rowan berries, on the soft mat of pine needles. They never made an arrangement. They met everywhere. To the young William she was a fairy tale. To both of them it was a game. Her mother had been alive then. She knew. She knew everything, and she said, "Janna, you must not do this."

But Janna shrugged her young shoulders. She was not doing anything; she was living. Her mother knew all about it and said no more.

The affair grew, like a big apple that becomes too heavy for the tree and falls to the ground with a plop. Just like that, it was suddenly over.

"Janna, it can't go on."

"I'm sorry, Janna, please understand."

"Janna . . . Janna . . . Janna. . . ."

The woods were empty, the trunk of the acacia was hard, the birds ate up the rowan berries, and the mat of pine needles was no longer a bed.

Longing, Janna had whitened her clogs and put up her hair in a hard knot. She must see him. Was there a place for a kitchen maid at the castle? But William did not want to see her anymore. Hadn't he said, "It's over. Go away"?

Old Janna, leaning against the tree, opened her eyes. What was she doing? Old loves, old sorrows. Go away, William with your black curls, rich William in the shining boots that another polishes for you, your house with the great windows full of light, the garden full of roses, and the woods full of game. A wild little girl from the woods can be thrown away, just like that. What was so precious that you wanted to hide it forever?

That had all happened long ago. Janna had lived through so much afterward. Surely that pain was past? Yet a long, long time went by before she had her own feelings under control and was able to put herself completely into the mind of the man whose companion she had been.

Then she started to walk again, past well-known trees that had grown so much older in the woods that were now tangled and unkempt. She came closer to the house. Her footsteps became heavier. Her face took on a different expression. She looked extraordinarily strange now, but no one saw her, and she was scarcely even aware of herself. Janna reached the wall. Brambles grew over it, and her clogs were still in the basket, left forgotten by the acacia, but she walked straight on. She felt none of the thorns that pricked her feet. She walked through the gap and into the garden like a sleepwalker. She narrowed her eyes to small slits, saw how it had been before, and felt what William had thought here. She nodded. This was the place, by the roses, of course. Not in the house and not in the woods.

Now Janna knew what she wanted to know, but she was not herself. She stopped quite still, eyes closed, in order to release the other personality gradually. And then there was someone standing before her. Go away, Janna, go away. It was not he. She grasped quickly enough who it was and laughed shrilly.

"You must look in the woods, deep in the woods, with a big spade," and she was gone.

William Vandyck stared in bewilderment. What on earth was that? An apparition? A strange old person in old-fashioned clothes with loose hair and bleeding feet, a witch. She had not touched the grass when she ran away and flitted over the wall. He ran after her but could see nothing. In the woods with a spade? What had she meant? He rubbed his eyes and went indoors.

Janna ran until she was out of breath, jumping over big tree trunks and pulling tough twigs loose. She was strong and felt a powerful triumph. She had found it! All she had to do was to return in the night, and she would find the treasure. But the young William, the new young William, wouldn't. He could dig the whole wood up with his spade. She laughed, loudly and harshly, with the sound of a fierce bird of prey. Then she slowed down a little. She found the basket and worked the thorns out of her feet. There was still some way to walk, but not until she saw William the crow on the lookout did she put her clogs on again. She tied back her hair and walked fairly normally into the yard. Chris was sitting in the sun, shelling beans.

"Hello, Janna. How did it go? Is your friend better?"

"It went well," said Janna, "very well. . . . There is no friend."

"Oh."

"But I know."

"What do you know?"

"I know where William hid his gold and silver. I know what he was thinking. I felt it. Hee-hee-hee, he should have known! He no longer needed Janna. He wanted another pleasure. Hee-hee-hee, what pleasure he had! First he buried his pennies, and then he himself was buried."

Chris thought her excited bleating sounded very disagreeable. "Janna, did you know the old baron?"

"Yes, indeed, I knew him. I knew him very well, but he never grew old, hee-hee-hee."

Chris was attacked by a terrible suspicion. "Janna, did you make him mad?"

Suddenly Janna's pleasure was over. "No, I did not do that. He did that himself. And you need not think that you know anything about it. You are just a little boy and can't understand anything. I did nothing. He went mad all on his own."

CHAPTER XII

Rain

"Alec."

"Yes, Grandpa."

"I've just been thinking it over again. How did it come about that great-grandfather's book was not in the little chest?"

By now Alec did not find it too difficult to tell him. Grandpa shook his white head. "I don't like it. You should not have done that."

"Well," said Alec, "but I didn't like it either when I was never allowed to look at it at all. You yourself said it was for me."

"Yes," said Grandpa, "I've been thinking about that. You're right. Look, here's another key to the little chest. You can have this, and we'll hang the cupboard key in a secret place. You can always take it without asking, but I shall count on your being just as careful with the books as I am."

"Yes, Grandpa."

Grandpa looked around the room. "What do you think? What would be a good place for a key?"

"In the kitchen drawer," said Alec. "There are so many bits and pieces in there that no one would notice the key."

But no, Grandpa did not think that was good enough. "Behind the cupboard, so that you can't see it, only feel it, and quite low down too—maybe eighteen inches off the ground."

Alec agreed, and Grandpa went to look for a copper hook in his toolbox and a drill of the right thickness. Now the cupboard had to be moved, and it was very heavy. They pulled and pushed together until, with a jerk, it suddenly moved forward.

"That will do."

The hand drill just fitted behind it. Grandpa drilled a hole and screwed the hook in. Then the cupboard was put back again, and sure enough the key was completely hidden there. So now Alec could open the cupboard himself and take out the books, but he didn't do it.

"Grandpa, shall I clean out the chicken coop?"

That was one of the jobs he always did when he was there for vacation. Today he was going to be home all day and would do everything for Grandpa. Alec was doing his best to recover the old intimacy, which had slipped away a little, unnoticed. Why? Because of the book? The exciting events in and around the castle? Chris?

He began to think about Chris, but he did not know

that the other boy was busy leading Bessie the cow to another meadow, just as he himself was chasing the last chicken, which did not want to go into the coop. All the others had gone for their feed like good chickens. At the same time as Chris was sweeping the threshing floor with Janna's big broom, Alec was brushing down Grandpa's little path. In the afternoon Alec helped to weed between the vegetable rows, and when Janna was coming home to meet Chris with a big basket of beans, Alec, too, was shelling beans on the seat in the sun while Grandpa peeled the potatoes.

The grassland began immediately beside the garden, and beyond you could see the Hazelhurst woods. Thick, white cloud banks rose above the woods.

"The weather is going to change," said Grandpa, and at that moment a rustling puff of wind chased through the trees. The weather had been hot and sunny for a full two weeks. They stayed outside, watching a heavy, gray sky mounting behind the white clouds. Not until the first big drops of rain began to fall did they go inside. A shattering storm burst overhead.

"That will refresh the garden," said Grandpa.

Together they watched the lightning flashes illuminating the woods strangely against the dark sky. Alec thought it was wonderfully beautiful. At last the storm gradually blew over, and only the pouring rain rattled against the windows. The water began to seep into the kitchen, and Grandpa put a bucket by the back door.

Then the beans were done, and they had their meal,

washed the dishes, and began to play games, which went on for a long time. Grandpa made hot chocolate twice, it went on raining, and things were almost exactly as usual.

The next day it was still raining. You couldn't play soccer or swim or go to the library here. There were generally all kinds of things to be done outside, but nothing at all inside. The house was tiny. There were no records or tapes to play—nothing.

Alec looked out the window at the back. The raindrops beat down on the currant bushes. Flip, flip went the leaves. He moved over to the front window. The begonia leaves were gleaming like metal, but the flowers were drooping. There was no window at the side; there you could hear the bubbling of the drainpipe. Grandpa had gone upstairs. Every day he wiped down the bedroom floors with a cloth knotted over the long mop. Alec had nothing to do. At last he went over to the cupboard.

For the first time he was holding the genuine old Auldland book in his hand. He had a very odd feeling. It was so old, older than almost anything else that existed. Well, of course, stones—a stone might be as old as the world—but they had no story to tell.

He turned page after page and saw the same hooked letters everywhere, no periods, no commas, or capitals. The whole story was a bore, he thought. No pictures. Oh, yes, there was one page with a kind of drawing on it. It did not look like anything, or perhaps it did look rather like North America. There were two more drawings of the same kind, one of them dirty and smeared.

There was Grandpa coming downstairs. He saw what Alec was doing and was going to tiptoe to the kitchen, but Alec asked, "Grandpa, what is this? Is it North America?"

"North America? That's possible. You may be right. There are more of those sketches at the back."

Grandpa showed him. They were different. Straight lines and curves, but these could not be maps.

"Sea charts perhaps? Oh, no," said Alec, "these must be the designs for their airships."

Once again Grandpa was filled with admiration. "You see much more in it than I do. I'm so glad that you've started on it now."

"But I just say the first thing that comes into my head. I don't know if it's true."

"You have imagination. I haven't. Keep on, look at everything, and tell me what you think."

Grandpa left him alone and went to the kitchen. Alec turned the pages. What was he supposed to think? Nothing. The book was full of letters that he couldn't read, and he didn't see very much in the mysterious drawings either. He had another look at North America. It did not fit at all, because in that case this other blob would have to be England, but it didn't look the least bit like it. It looked like a cauliflower. He closed the book and looked at the other things in the little chest. The schoolmaster's papers. A vocabulary list: sun, house, ship, land, moon, baggage or food, a period (year or longer?). Pretty bright of the schoolmaster. Alec looked out the window. It was raining. And Grandpa was in the garden! In a shiny black raincoat. He must be going to see what had become of the strawberries. Strawberry mousse. And this was a letter mousse.

He would look again another time and make Chris happy. He must find out what Chris thought about it. Alec's imagination had run out. He packed the books away tidily and locked everything up. Then he got out his boots and a jacket. Strawberries, raspberries, half-ripe apples, yum!

Janna's farm lay among the trees like a fairy-tale house. The thatched roof was like a tall wig, hitched up over each window. The panes sparkled; the dark shutters gleamed. Under their own roof the pigeons sat huddled together. The rain laid a silver net over everything. William was not perched on the well. When Chris walked across the threshing floor, the crow came to meet him. His dry, hard claws tapped on the uneven floor, and he looked up with bright, intelligent eyes.

"Do you want to join us, William? Come in."

When Janna was not outside working, she almost always sat in the little kitchen, but she was not there now. Was she out in the rain after all? Or in the barn? William walked straight across the kitchen to the door behind the stove. That was where the big kitchen was, a spacious, chilly, north-facing room, where they never sat. Chris eased the door open a crack, and William slipped through. Yes, there she was, standing on a foot stove in front of the open cabinet.

"Come in here," said Janna. "I want to show you something."

She stepped off the foot stove and pushed up a chair. The cabinet was high, and Janna was quite small."When I am dead, it will all be yours," said Janna. "But you had better know what I keep in here. This is a good day for it." She tugged at a thick roll of cloth. "Here, get hold of this."

Chris had to lay the roll on the table, and then another one.

"It's behind there," said Janna. "Anyone could find it, but after all nobody comes here."

She pulled a little wooden chest toward her. Chris had to put it on the table. Then came a round basket, and after that Janna stepped down again. The little chest had a lid that slid back on runners.

"Look," said Janna. There were five limp dolls inside. Chris thought they were made of flax, with clothes of some very old material.

"They're made of hair. This is my mother."

"Oh."

"And when I'm dead you must make a doll for me too. You must cut off my hair and braid it. I shall teach you how to do it with sheep's wool. If I am bald, you can use wool, but then you must include a few nail clippings. You stick the eyes on with beeswax. Remember, you mustn't forget. You must make the clothes from clothes I have actually worn."

"Okay," said Chris, "where are the scissors?"

"You don't need them yet. I've no intention of dying just now."

"That's lucky, but I've never seen a pair of scissors here yet. That's why I was asking."

Janna stroked the dress of the doll that was her mother. She had the same black, beady eyes as William, who sat watching on the back of a chair.

"What is it for, Janna?"

"Perhaps you may think of me sometimes when I am dead."

"Of course."

"Well, that's what it's for. You pick up the doll, and I will be there. You don't have to believe it. You don't have to believe anything, as long as you do it."

She returned her mother carefully to the other dolls in the chest. "Hair and beeswax, remember. Later I will tell you more. And now this."

In the basket she had a piece of wood, a snippet of crochet work, and a thin, gray book.

"Oh, Janna, a book!"

"It's not a book to read. An old Gypsy gave it to me when I was traveling with the crows. The lines of the palm are in it. Long life, a friend from abroad, that kind of thing. And this is a letter that Mihaela sent me when I was young."

Chris knew how a snippet of crochetwork could be a letter. The members of the association sent messages to each other that way. Each different stitch meant something else, such as time or distance. You could tell a great

many things with quite a little scrap. Chris had already
learned how to do it, and he knew Mihaela too. She was
the chief woman in the association, lined and terribly old,
perhaps the oldest woman in the world. She had wanted
to see Chris.

"You never told me what happened with Mihaela," said
Janna.

"You know quite well I can't," said Chris.

"There are things you could say."

"Yes."

"Your father had to go to Rumania."

"Yes, and he was going to take me, and I wanted to see
Mihaela, but I didn't even know exactly where she lived."

"And you found her yourself," Janna prompted Chris.

"Yes. We were camping by the River Olt, and there
was a spring where we always got water. A little boy used
to come and get water too. His arms and legs were very
thin and the bucket was very heavy, so I helped him. The
water was for a blind woman, and I knew at once who it
was. We were there for almost two weeks, and I carried
water to her every day, but I never talked to her because
we did not know each other's language."

"I knew that already," said Janna, "but all the same she
told you everything. I know her. I know how she does it."

"Yes," said Chris, "without words." And he thought to
himself, I must not use the stone. For a whole year I must
never use the stone, but I am allowed to keep it with me.

Of course, Mihaela had said more. But those thoughts
had been meant for him and not for Janna, however

much she wanted to know, and that was why he said only, "What else is there in the basket?" Janna was at the same time a wise and a very unwise woman. She had not always used her art well. And Mihaela had particularly wanted to meet him in order to know whether he could stand up to her.

"Runes," said Janna, "a bone with runes on it."

She took the last object out of the basket. It was not wood, but a piece of bone, brown with age, with complicated marks burned into it. "This is for you too, when I am dead," she said mournfully.

"Dear Janna, couldn't you take a long time about it?" said Chris, putting one arm around her. "First you will have to be as old as Mihaela, and if you are blind I will look after the pigeons."

"I can't grow as old as that. I haven't that much power. I have only a little, and you already have more by now."

She had believed that she could catch him out. She had failed, and now she was disappointed.

"I have a little power sometimes," said Chris, "but there is much I have to learn. Janna, please stay here a long time."

"Okay," said Janna, using one of Chris's words for the first time. She held the piece of bone in her thin, old hand and said, "If you think these are letters, you have it all wrong. A rune is the sign of a power with which the world was made. The fire, the beginning, the deed. For every power there is a rune."

CHAPTER XIII

'Friends

Janna taught Chris how to make a binding rune, through which powers strengthen each other, and still the rain kept on falling. The green, velvety moss on the roof swelled up, the grass grew firmer, the thirsty wood drank and drank.

The rain fell on the castle too, even inside it in some places. *Plop, plop,* drips on a wooden floor, *plink, plink,* a leak in the kitchen. A gutter overflowed, making a raging waterfall on one balcony. The peaceful shushing on the roof was drowned in all kinds of tappings and babblings, like a musical performance.

William Vandyck was unable to listen to it with pleasure. He had a look at the leaks but had nothing to put under them. Then he retreated into the bedroom, which really was beginning to become his room. There he slept under his old camping blanket, there he brought in more and more things: a table and a mug, a small tape recorder, and a pile of books. He began to read but could not stop trying to make out where that little splashing came from. Yet another leak? At last he closed his book, put on his thin raincoat, climbed on the yellow bicycle, and rode into the village. The coat did not help him much. He was soaking wet in a moment.

When the peanut-butter sandwiches became really dull, he ate at The Thirsty Stag, the old village hostelry. Outside hung an inn sign showing the stag, wild with thirst. Through a wide glass door you entered a dark hall, where the coat hooks consisted of large antlers. The tap-room, or whatever it was called, was cozy. There was a huge bar made up of a thousand small panels. The bottles above it were almost all empty. And you could not choose what you wanted to eat from a menu. All they had was steak or chops and occasionally fish. But the owner's wife could cook a very decent meal. Sometimes there were one or two other customers, but not today. After all, it was still very early.

Naturally the people here knew exactly who William was and also what he had come to do, but that did not bother him. William would never discuss family matters with strangers. He had found it difficult enough with Miss Roterdink, and she was almost a member of the family.

The owner of the inn would very much have liked to chat, but he got no farther than the weather with this silent guest.

"That's no shower out there, sir."

"Indeed."

"But the land really needed it."

"I believe you."

"And the woods too, sir. It's a pity that nothing is ever done for them."

"A pity, yes," said William. To himself, he thought, Hold your tongue, man. It's a pity about my house, a pity about my poor uncle, who never married. A pity, pity, pity, and it's also a pity about the steak that is finished. Bah, I'm going to leave this place. I shall never find those coins.

The old witch had said, "Look in the woods." And with a spade, preferably. She certainly had made an impression on him. But he had already looked when the weather was fine, and he could imagine what a cheerless state it would all be in now. In the sunshine William had not wanted to give up. He had come here to escape the dismal rain and to eat properly for once, and now this deadly innkeeper was beginning to remind him of all the misery with his chatter. He accepted defeat.

"What time does the bus go? Can I leave my bike here for a few days?"

He paid, reluctantly put on the soaking raincoat again, and went to Leiden. Later on he would probably come and pick up his things. He would find a real-estate agent quickly and be done with the whole thing.

He arrived late in the evening. It was vacation time. None of his friends would be in their pubs now, but that was not too important. In Leiden it was not as late as it would be in the country at the same time. There were Guy and Tim, Louis and Bo. And Barbara, Saskia, and Greta too.

"Hi, William, how did you get on at the ancestral castle?"

"Dreary," said William. "I'm going to sell it as quickly as possible."

He had told no one why he had gone there, had not mentioned his Aunt Reine's letter. Now he sat there, beaten, and Guy tried to cheer him up.

"If you're so upset about it, there may be another solution. Couldn't you just sell the land? Or rent the house in summer, for conferences to be held in, and so on? That would be sure to bring in enough for the maintenance."

"It's not even a question of that. I can't talk to the people there."

"What on earth does that matter? You're fed up with the weather, my boy. I understand. There you sat, miles from the inhabited world, with only the natives around you and endless pouring rain. Just you wait until the sun shines again. Then it will all look different."

"You don't understand. There should be something else there, something that which used to belong to my uncle, and I'm convinced that the farmer knows about it, but he's as closemouthed as an oyster. I asked and asked and I've looked everywhere myself, but I got nowhere. I'm sick of it."

"What were you looking for? What did your uncle have there?"

"A coin collection."

Uncle William had been the man you didn't mention, the one who put the family to shame. In his defeated state, William no longer cared. He told Guy more than he had ever told anyone before. And it soon appeared that someone else could look at the thing from quite a different angle. A fabulously rich recluse with a hobby for which he dissipated the entire family capital, for which he traveled to London in a track suit, that was too much for Guy.

"Listen, you guys, you've got to hear this. Tim and Bo, William's uncle—"

"Oh, no," said William.

"Now don't sulk, my boy."

William was much too sleepy to sulk.

Ancient coins, farms sold off. The story silenced them for a moment, but that did not last long.

"How many farms?"

"How should I know?"

"Did he have drachmae? Did he have a fifteenth-century groat?"

"William, was there an obol among them?"

"He had everything—bent and crooked, made of leather and iron and unusual alloys—the oldest coins in existence, struck in Asia three thousand years ago. I would really love to have found them, but I can't see doing it now."

"Well, I *can* see doing it. Have you got a guest room there, William?"

"How much are you asking for the old barracks? Can I buy it from you? Then the pickings will be mine."

"Only a filthy egoist like Tim could have said that.
That won't do. It's all for William, and we all get ten
percent."

"Ha ha ha, ha ha."

"But how do you know it's still there?"

"I don't know. That's just the point. But, at any rate, the
rarest items have never turned up anywhere else. Of course
it's possible that the farmer found them and melted them
down because the money is no longer currency."

"You must find out."

"How? The man says nothing."

"We'll go with you. We'll fix it for you. Naturally you
went about it with velvet gloves. We'll apply the iron
hand."

"We'll get some police uniforms at the theater and go
through him with a fine-toothed comb."

"I'll catch him when you've softened him up, Bo," said
Greta, "and then he'll tell me his secrets."

"The people there are quite different from what you
think," said William. "A policeman's uniform would make
no impression at all on Slot, and Greta's mascara wouldn't
either."

"We'll go all the same," said Greta, "and I don't even
need your spare room. I'll go in the tent with Louis."

"Do that," said William wearily. He heaved himself to
his feet and trudged listlessly to his room. He left the raincoat behind, for the rain was over.

CHAPTER XIV

An
Ailing
Foot

"Is there much to do when it's been raining?" asked
Chris. He felt like going out again. Perhaps Alec might
have read something in the book, perhaps there were
magic spells in it that they could try out together. Chris
was very keen on magic. He had practiced it himself, once
or twice, when he had just acquired the magic stone. Afterward the members of the association had quickly taken
over, and Mihaela. He had to abide by what Mihaela had
taught him, Chris had no doubt about that. Later on he
had discussed the whole matter fully with his friend Frank's
grandmother, who was another wise old woman. You must
not make use of powers you do not know, because you
can't foresee the consequences. It was as simple as that.

An now he was apprenticed to Janna, who lived so close
to nature that she could show him the powers. And the
stone stayed safe in his pocket. He was not allowed to use
it; he did not use it. He had almost forgotten that magic
existed.

But then Alec had come, Alec with his grandpa's book. If they used one of the magic spells from it, that would be quite different. It could do no harm, and it was at least a change from being good and obedient.

"Is there much to do when it's been raining?"

"Naturally," said Janna. "Preserving. All the fruit that has been damaged has to be preserved before it goes rotten."

Chris had to climb the plum trees, pick up baskets of apples, shell beans. And Janna stood in front of the fire, stirring the big black pans and smoking the jars clean with sulphur.

It was "Go and fetch this. Get on and do that." And all the time she said, "Faster, faster, faster."

"You'd do better to teach me to fly first," said Chris discontentedly. "I'm doing my best, aren't I?"

Janna almost let her spoon slide into the jam. "But that's just what I'm teaching you! Faster and faster, think yourself to the place where you want to be, and you will rise off the ground."

"Oh, yes," said Chris.

"You don't have to believe it. You don't have to believe anything, if only you'll do it." She went over to the table to get a skimmer, not as fast as flight, but painfully, limping.

"Janna, what's wrong with your foot?"

"Nothing at all. It will be better tomorrow—or tonight. Then I have to go somewhere. It might be a good thing if you picked a few plantain leaves."

Chris went outside. Beside the well grew some plantain,

with its thin brown candles. Janna took off her thick woolen stocking. Her left foot was red and puffy: inflamed.

"That's because I stepped on those thorns. In the old days I always went barefoot. My feet could stand anything then, but those days are gone. Bah, they've gone soft."

"You must soak them in soda," said Chris.

"Soda? That will make them softer still. Will you stir for a minute?"

Chris set the hot red pulp in motion and looked around to see what Janna was doing. She packed a thick layer of leaves on the inflamed area and replaced her stocking over them.

"It has to be better tonight."

"If you want to go out tonight, you will have to fly because the bicycle is wrecked. Otherwise I would take you."

She gave him a vexed look. "In the old days I could nearly fly. I was very light. But I never learned to do it properly because there was always something I wanted to do more. And now it's no use. But you don't have to take me."

Suddenly Chris knew what she wanted to do: search, of course. She had said that she knew where William had hidden his gold and silver. Was it really gold and silver? Would she find it? And keep it herself? Alec and he would have liked to find it too. And what then? He had not thought that far, but Janna had, for sure. Oh, well, her foot would not be better by tonight, anyway.

Janna began to stir her jam again, and Chris went out

to the bean patch. He kept on thinking of "William's gold and silver." What did Janna want with it? Nothing, probably, since money meant little to her. She just wanted to be too clever for everyone, especially the young Hazelhurst, who was so like the William of old. He would not put it past her to have thought up a malicious plan, and he was more and more determined to be ahead of Janna.

As Chris dropped the ripe beans in the basket one by one, he was dreaming up a whole episode. He was with Alec, reading the magic book. Alec thought it was nonsense, Grandpa did not understand it, but Chris would say, "If you just look at it like this. . . ." Alec would say, "Come now," and Grandpa would give him a thoughtful look and say, "That's possible."

He left out the next part for the time being, because he had absolutely no idea what might be in the book, but in any case Alec and he would find the rottentooth and they would find the treasure too. They would first look at it in peace at home, and only afterward would they fetch the man with the big feet. "Take a look at this. What do you think?" Of course they would be given a reward. What would he give them? A bicycle! No doubt about it, Alec and he would get one each—perhaps even a racing bike with ten gears and a water bottle. And one of those funny round bags behind the saddle. Okay, keep on!

While Chris was daydreaming he went on picking beans calmly, but some of them had spoiled already. Under the hard pod was a soggy mess that stuck to his fingers.

Then Janna would come out. "Is your foot better already, Janna? Where do you have to go in the night? After William's treasure? Oh, but that's no longer necessary. We've found it already."

Well, it wouldn't be quite like that, but all the same it would be great if he could show Janna that he could do a thing or two, that he really was something better than a curly-headed boy who could be used to pick beans and comb wool. And she would also see that you *could* learn something from a book. Chris wanted the part he had imagined for Janna to come true most of all. It was a good thing she had a sore foot.

Both of them worked hard all day long. Now and then it rained a little more, but by evening a big orange sun hung behind the oak trees, and they were able to sit outside, Janna with her foot up. She packed it in some fresh leaves.

"It has gone down," she said hopefully, but Chris could not see it. She could walk on it, yes, but not far. The inflammation was sure to last a few more days, he thought. The problem was to get away from here. If Janna knew that he wanted to see Alec, she would prevent him. She had already done so today. There was enough work on the little farm for years.

CHAPTER XV

Turnips

The day after the great rainfall Alec dawdled about, hoping that Chris would come again. First he looked for fruit in the garden. Then he searched under all the trees for gray threads, but he could not see them, and there was another shower coming. He took refuge in the garden shed. There were Grandpa's tools. Should he try to make something? The birdhouse he had begun with Grandpa was still there. A little bit had to be shaved off the side because the roof did not fit very well as it was. But in order to plane it off he would have to take the house to pieces again. Alec turned it over and over. He didn't dare do it. It was all lopsided now. He would never be able to get it back together again. How awful if the bottom fell out just as the little birds started to live in it!

The shower stopped, and he went out again. Was Chris coming? He went to the front of the house, across the doll-size yard and, *squeak, clack,* through the gate, across the road. To the left was the village, to the right the castle, and no other way to go. A small world.

Still smaller was the world of the roadside. He squatted to look: grass, thin, pointed leaves, smooth, round leaves, dark, shiny, and serrated leaves covered with down, flying, creeping, and crawling creatures. He wondered whether there was a name for every little creature. There were people who bothered about such things, but not Alec: Fly or worm was name enough for him. Beetle was all right too. A bright red beetle was climbing up his sleeve. He wished he could go vertically upward like that. Easy, if you had six legs. And this silly thing had wings as well. Had the Aulders really been able to fly? Alec did not know what to think. Chris believed it. He looked to the left and right. No sign of Chris. But there was a tractor, heavy and snorting, with an empty wagon behind it. The farmer driving it was Henry Rengerink, whom he had been allowed to help from time to time, and suddenly Alec had no desire to go on wandering around pointlessly, waiting to see if Chris were coming or not.

"Can I come along, Henry?"

"Jump up." Alec took a run and hoisted himself onto the back of the muddy wagon.

"Where are you going?"

"To pull turnips in the quarter-acre."

"I can pull turnips."

"Come along then."

Alec was entirely happy. Doing real work was the best thing he knew, and the fact that it made you incredibly filthy, especially when it had just been raining, made it all the more real. He was no longer thinking about Chris.

The piece of land known as the quarter-acre was some way off, right against the northern edge of the Hazelhurst woods. They drove past the castle, and after a long, clattering stretch they had to turn off down a bumpy path with low bushes along either side. The turnip field was small. Henry's old Volkswagen was standing there, and his son Gerry was working on it with Tom, his wife's brother. Alec was told to pull out the turnips along the sloping side of the field. He was allowed to drive the tractor too, but only straight ahead, and at the edge of the field he had to get down. Gerry drove on, and his father loaded the wagon. The brother worked some way behind them. He said not a word, and Alec thought there was something strange about him, but he didn't know what. Later on he noticed that the man spoke very indistinctly. He probably thinks differently from other people, Alec observed to himself, or perhaps just a bit less.

After about an hour, Henry took out a packet of bread and a thermos with coffee. They went and sat under a big tree in the corner of the field, because it was raining slightly again.

"The wifie is over there," said Tom. Henry and Gerry went on chewing their sandwiches in silence.

"Which wifie?" asked Alec.

"A big wifie."

Alec looked questioningly at the other two, but they stared straight ahead, grinding their jaws. Henry poured out the coffee. He had three handleless cups, one for Alec, one for brother Tom, and he himself shared the third with Gerry. Tom slobbered his coffee, taking a big gulp, and beginning to talk with his mouth full. Alec could not understand a word he said, and the others were obviously not in the habit of taking any notice of him. He stopped talking and went on staring somberly ahead. Alec thought him pathetic.

They worked on for half an hour, until the wagon was full.

"What do you want to do, Alec, come in the Volkswagen or with the load?"

"With the load."

It was still drizzling, but Alec thought it was much more fun to ride in the open wagon behind the tractor than in an ordinary car. Gerry laid an old sack over the muddy load. Alec was not wearing his jacket. His hands were black. He had wiped them on his face and also on his trousers and sleeves. The bottoms of his trousers were soaked through. It doesn't matter, thought Alec. It's not cold. He pushed himself higher up so that he was sitting directly on the wet turnips, for the sack had slipped a little. He watched the tractor jolting ahead of him. There was too much noise to be able to talk to Henry.

In front of Grandpa's cottage Henry stopped the tractor. "Thanks, Alec. So long."

"So long," Alec called, "and thank you too." He jumped down from the wagon, pushed the little gate open, and ran around to the back and in through the kitchen door.

"Hi, Grandpa! I've been helping Henry. Has Chris been here?"

"Alec, how you look!"

"Oh, well, it doesn't matter."

"It does," said Grandpa. "I don't want a fuss from the woman who comes to clean up here. Go take a shower right away."

Grandpa had a little shower stall upstairs, but he didn't use it every day and neither did Alec. Instead, he used the washbowl and if he had dirty feet, which was every day, of course, he had to stand on a chair to get his feet into it. In the shower was a bucket, a step stool, and a basin, all of which had to be removed before Alec could get in. Grandpa went upstairs with him, and there was a tremendous to-do. First Alec's clothes had to go in the bucket. Alec had the feeling that he had done something wrong, and yet all he had done was help and have a good time. Only when he was sitting, quite clean and with flattened hair, in the garden with a bowl of raspberries did Grandpa behave normally again, and then he was able to ask him the question that had been puzzling him.

"Grandpa, what's the matter with Henry's brother?"

"His brother-in-law. Nothing. He couldn't keep up at school, but he can work very well."

"He said that there is 'a wifie' in the woods. What could he mean? A wifie is a woman, isn't it?"

"He must have met someone. Perhaps that Janna you were talking about."

"Oh, yes." Alec thought about it. "A big wifie," Tom

had said. And Janna smoked a pipe. She might easily be a
bit mannish. Alec had gained the impression that Tom
didn't mean some ordinary woman, and Janna was certainly not ordinary. He himself would very much like to
go and have a look at her one day.

Alec leaned back in his chair and gazed at the sky. The
weather was improving. He swallowed one raspberry after
another as he sat thinking. After the rain there would be
no bicycle tracks left, and he had gone astray the first
time. He could only go if he scattered pebbles or unwound
a ball of wool, the way people did in fairy tales. And if he
found Janna's house he would creep behind the hedge.
There was always a hedge at a farm, but of course there
would be a dog too. A woman like that, who didn't want
to see anyone, would have a dog that barked when you
were half a mile away, like those great wild animals of
Farmer Slot's. Would it be better not to go? What then?
If he went to help Henry again, Grandpa would be difficult. Problem. Oops, the last raspberry.

Oh-oh, now they were finished. He should have played
a counting-out game with them: Chris, Henry, Chris,
Henry. And the last fruit would be the choice he would
make. "Grandpa, could I have some more raspberries?"

He had to wait until the meal was over, and by then the
game was no longer necessary. Alec had made a decision.
He would stay at home next morning because Chris
might come to see him. But if Chris was not there by one
o'clock, he would start to walk through the woods with
a big bag of pebbles. He would practice finding his way

back a few times, and then he would go farther and farther. He might find a house. Perhaps that house would have in it a big wifie who smoked a pipe, and then it was also possible that he would find Chris there. That was how it would be.

CHAPTER XVI

Janna's House

When Janna removed the bandage next morning, her foot was almost well again.

"It does look much better," said Chris, surprised.

"Naturally. Plantain leaves, just remember that. I shall be able to go out this evening. And now you must look for a little plant for me. It looks like hedge parsley, but the stalks are red, with fine, dark hairs. I need them for my pipe."

Janna didn't smoke every day, but now she had a fancy to it because smoking would take her mind off her foot, which she wanted to use as much as possible, "because," she said, "if the foot keeps moving, the blood keeps going through it, and that's good for it." She described the plant precisely and also the place where it would probably be growing.

Now I can go, thought Chris. I can act as if I had trouble finding it and go quickly to Alec and back, because if Janna is going tonight we have to hurry.

All the same he looked for the place Janna had spoken

of and found the plant at once. He picked a few leaves and sniffed at them—a strong fragrance. Janna always said that every plant did something, and the fragrant ones did most of all. He would bring it to her right away. The walk to Alec's and back again would take him three hours, and he did not want to do it that way. Chris had lived too long and too deeply in the world of powers, where a lie is pointless. He would have to come right out with it: "Janna, I'm going out. See you tonight."

Chris took Janna the leaves but said nothing. Was the plan with the rottentooth too vague and fantastic? Was he curious to see what Janna would do with the herb? Or was he perhaps afraid of her after all?

Chris stayed close to home all day, which was why things were able to turn out exactly as Alec had imagined, except of course that Janna was-not a big wifie but a scrawny little woman.

He had a big bag of pebbles with him, gravel, which he had hastily scraped up from Miss Roterdink's garden when she had gone around to the back to hang up the washing, but he did not need it at once. He still remembered the way he had gone last time, and he recognized the place where he had met Chris. He also saw a crow again and later another one. The crows had human eyes, Alec thought. He watched which way they were flying. The woods were no longer so dense here. He saw that the birds made a wide arc, but a long way off they turned, and he could just make out the tiny black specks heading for a darker patch.

Chris had said nothing about crows. Alec did not know

that they were spies for Janna, who guarded her seclusion very fiercely. When they let her know that an unknown person was approaching, she sent them back again. Then they would lead the stranger away from the path to her house, or if that did not work, they would actually threaten him with their sharp beaks. But this morning Janna was sitting rather stuffily by the stove in her kitchen and Chris received the crows outside. He gave them some crumbs instead of urging them on as Janna generally did, so Alec walked on, undisturbed, toward the darker patch, dropping a pebble from time to time. When he was close to it, it still looked like no more than a darker patch, but suddenly he saw that it was a thick grove of old oaks. And he saw a little apple tree there too, and cabbages and leeks and rich red currants.

I have found it, thought Alec, and he was right. He walked past a sturdy elder, and there stood the house, wide and low under a cozy thatched roof on which moss and small ferns grew. The square panes reflected darkly between the white-painted frames. Beside the well was a big wheel, which squeaked and groaned. Chris was turning it, hauling up a bucket of water. There was no dog, but there were geese, which advanced threateningly on Alec. The crows were not pleased to see him there either. The pigeons began to look restless, and even the hens appeared unfriendly.

After all his trouble, Alec thought it would be silly to be driven off by a few fowls. He put his hand in the bag of pebbles. He would give them a fright.

Chris saw him. He began to laugh but said quickly, "Don't do it, Alec. Don't throw them."

The door opened, out came a little witch, and sure enough she had a smoking pipe. "Get 'em, William. Gertie, Ginny, chase 'em off!"

"No, Janna," said Chris, "this is Alec. He's my friend. Come on, Alec."

Alec just managed not to run away, but he didn't dare take another step.

"I don't need your friends," cried Janna shrilly, but she no longer set the animals on him and left Alec unharmed. Chris picked up a branch that was lying under the elder bush and gently drove the hens and geese away. The crows sat on the well to watch.

"I've had a meal with Alec's grandpa," said Chris. "Surely we can give Alec some tea?"

"There's no need for him to think I keep a tearoom," she said tartly, going indoors. She was old and at the same time young in the way she moved. Grandpa was slow and a bit stiff, but this little woman walked with light, rapid steps. She came back again at once, carrying a tray and three mugs. They were old mugs with a thousand little cracks all over them, but the handles were still there. The tea was green. Alec did not know what to do with himself. Janna went on staring at him with her narrow, fierce, little eyes. He scarcely dared to drink his tea, but when he saw Chris doing so he took a gulp himself.

"He's no good to you," Janna told Chris. "He can neither see nor hear."

Alec thought, Is she talking about me?

"But he did find your house, Janna," said Chris.

"Yes, that's true. Could you see it? Did you see the light above the trees?"

"I saw a darker patch," said Alec, "and the crows were flying this way."

"You see, he can't see. And you can't see Chris's light either, I suppose?"

Alec did not know what she meant. No, he could see no light.

Janna nodded eagerly. "Just as I thought. Here, have some more tea."

Alec thought the tea was very good, and the cookie she gave him was good too.

"You can have another one," said Janna, "as long as you don't get the idea that I keep a restaurant. You'll be off soon, no doubt. You'll have a long way to walk."

"Okay," said Alec, standing up at once. "Good-bye. Thank you for the tea."

Janna burst into fits of laughter.

"I'll go a little way with you," Chris said.

"You don't have to. I can find it." Alec wanted to get as far away as possible now. At that moment he was not particularly eager to have a chat with Chris.

Then Janna said, "What is it you want from him? That book, I suppose. He's the boy with the book, isn't he? Well, it's no use to either of you. I know quite well what sort of a book it is. You can't read it."

"That's true," said Alec, "but I'm going to learn the language."

"Hee-hee-hee-hee! Even if you know the language, you still won't know what it says. No use. There's no point in your reading it, because you still won't understand it, and if you did understand it, you wouldn't need the book. Off you go, look at it together. There are letters in it, dead letters with no power. Power! You don't need anything else." She picked up the tray with the mugs on it and went into the house.

Chris walked beside Alec in silence. When they had gone a little way, he began to talk. "I'm glad you came. I wanted to go and see you, but I couldn't get away. And I'm glad Janna has seen you too. What do you think of her?"

Alec stared at Chris. Janna had given him quite a hard time, but he didn't know what to say. "I really don't understand why you like being there," he said at last.

"No, of course not," said Chris, "and I don't really know either, but I do like it. It's a nice place. When I'm at home, I often think of Janna's homestead and it always makes me feel better. And Janna herself is much nicer than she seems. Most people are the other way around. They act sweet and don't mean it. Janna's always better than you expect."

"Oh." Alec was thinking, What must it be like at Chris's house? Is it perfectly all right with them for him to spend so long with that crazy woman? "Do you know what Grandpa said?" he went on. "You may always look in the book, and I may too. I have the key to the little chest."

Chris was elated. "But too bad you haven't got it with

you! We need it." Then he told the story of Janna and
the baron. "She thinks she knows where the money is,
and she wants to go and hunt for it tonight. That's why
we really have to have the rottentooth now, to get ahead
of her."

"Rottentooth? What are you talking about?"

Oh, yes, of course. For a moment Chris had forgotten
that Alec was someone from the ordinary world, where
magic arts did not exist, where everything that did not
happen in a straightforward way, through an ordinary
action, was "accidental." Chris should have read the book
at Alec's house, asked about the cooked friend, and then
suggested innocently, "Shall we try it? Just for fun? Perhaps we'll find the treasure!" And if Alec had not agreed,
he could have tried alone, once he had read what
to do. But now he had let the cat out of the bag. If he
were to go on, Alec would think him as nutty as a fruit-
cake. Oh, well, it was too late anyway.

"Oh, nothing," said Chris, "I made a mistake."

The sun was shining again. Two blue butterflies were
dancing around the gleaming needles of a spruce fir. The
treasure isn't important, thought Chris. If I find it, it's
not for me. It will be old and dusty and probably sad too.
Let it lie. If Janna finds it, okay. Just give me a spruce
tree in the sunshine. And he became very cheerful, because he had been able to think that way.

"I read a bit in the book," said Alec, "about the cooked
friend. I know it by heart."

"Oh," said Chris, "oh, yes? Come on, tell me."

"Let me think." Alec shut his eyes and stood still with his hands behind his back. "To find this friend you must first be freshly washed." He opened his eyes again. "I am. Grandpa made me go under the shower. Also you must be light of heart."

Chris nodded. It always had to be like that when you were looking for herbs or doing anything with magic.

"Then should you walk. . . ." Alec hesitated from time to time, and halfway through he had to begin again from the beginning, but he really did know the whole story. "And I asked Grandpa if he had ever found gray threads," he finished, "but he has never looked for them. Funny, isn't it, when he believes everything in that book? But I believe your Janna is right: If you know what's there, you still don't understand it. That's why Grandpa has never been able to do anything with it."

"Say that bit about the sun and the roots again."

It fits exactly, Chris was thinking. Gray threads. Janna said the rottentooth looked like moss and was a fungus. He looked around. A "fruit-bearing tree": elder, rowan, juniper, an acorn was actually a fruit too, so was a fir cone. Perhaps it was not too late after all. The spruce fir at the edge of the woods had looked so healthy and cheerful. The sun shone brightly, and the shadows were growing longer. Perhaps, perhaps he would still find the fungus.

"Do you think you know the way yourself from now on?"

"Of course. I dropped pebbles."

There were smooth white stones on the path and a delicate feather as well. Alec stooped. He saw a gray-green film on the wrinkled root of a young silver birch. "Look, gray threads. There they are. But no, a birch doesn't have fruit."

"It does. Those thin, flaky catkins are the fruit of the birch, and it's not tainted."

Chris stroked the silky skin of the trunk. "That's it. No doubt about it. Can you see that they are tiny toadstools?"

The moist threads were thicker below than above, and on the top sat a little hat, like a pinhead, which was even thinner than the stalk.

"I'll take some with me for Grandpa."

"I'd like a few too."

Alec took out his handkerchief and gently placed a small handful of the delicate plants on it. Chris took up a piece of moss and laid some on it. Then each went his own way.

"Perhaps I'll come tomorrow," said Chris.

CHAPTER XVII

Rottentooth

Alec walked through the silent woods, the questions chiming inside his head. The woods were not really silent. The birds were singing, tweeting, hooting, and whistling, but all in a calm, peaceful way, which made the surroundings just right for thinking. In the short time that Alec had known Chris a whole lot of questions had come up in his mind: What was Janna? What was Chris doing there? What was he, himself? Now he was faced with the same questions, but within an hour or two they had grown enormously. On the surface, Chris seemed an ideal friend, happy, never cross, and able to think up all kinds of things. But he kept a great deal of himself hidden—now more than ever.

Why did Chris need his book? What was rottentooth, and why had he suddenly said no more? Alec had no desire for a friendship with someone who seemed to be holding out on him. When Chris came tomorrow, he would have to tell him exactly what he had really meant just now. As far as Janna was concerned, he could tell Alec about her or not, as he wished, but if it concerned something in Grandpa's book, he must put his cards on the table. And yet Alec found Janna the most difficult thing of all. Possibly she was nicer than she seemed, but he would prefer not to have a fight with her. He found her a scary person. How fierce she was, with her dead letters. Had anyone ever heard of live letters? And power! Alec was thinking of the book again. Appearances are deceptive; powers make up the real world.

He looked about him. What were you left with, if this warm, peaceful woods was not real? How could you live if you could not believe in what you saw? Janna had said of him: he can neither see nor hear. Then did she and Chris see things that other people did not see? Grandpa had said, "If you believe what no one else believes, you have a poor life." Alec Aulder of two hundred years ago, going to church to save his life. Were they perhaps no longer burning heretics in 1761, but still burning witches? Burning people, horrible. But a world that is there and that you cannot see is horrible too.

Alec was well able to understand the fear that simple, ordinary people had of witches, who could make use of invisible powers and did so, who could do harm invisibly. Had they all been killed in earlier times, apart from Janna's great-great-grandmother and his great-great-grandfather? And when there was no one left to practice magic, no one believed in it. Witches do not exist, they have never existed, magic is not true. And meanwhile the "powers" have always remained, in the deepest secrecy, far away in a dark wood, and in a book in a little iron chest in the cupboard with the locked door in the house of Alec's own grandfather.

Alec had worked himself into a misery. He stared suspiciously at the swaying tip of a tall spruce, the deep shadow under a bird cherry covered with honeysuckle. In a lighter spot he unfolded the handkerchief and looked at his "gray threads." They were already limp, no longer so pretty. Shall I throw them away? thought Alec. His distaste for all those horrid thoughts made him find the little fungus distasteful too. But he kept it all the same, for Grandpa.

Now he was close to the castle. The path across the garden was much shorter than the one past the farm, but the man with the yellow bicycle did not want him to walk across the garden. What was he to do? Alec peered through the gap in the wall. He couldn't see if the bicycle was there, but he heard something. Noise, shouts, loud laughter. A lot of people were there. Alec moved away from the wall and chose the path past the barking dogs.

He wondered what was going on at the castle. Had the yellow bicycle man sent for reinforcements? Perhaps they were at this very moment laying rows of sleeping bags on the bare wooden floors. And tomorrow they would go into the woods together, each with a spade over his shoulder, to hunt for the treasure. But Janna would have been before them, because she was going tonight, and Chris had said she knew where to go. And Chris would be ahead of her in his turn, if only he had had the book and—what was it? Rottentooth? Suddenly the thought struck Alec, "Perhaps that's what I've got in my hand. Perhaps it's not such a silly story after all." He repeated it all over again to himself, taking another look at the already thinner, drying threads. Should he cook them? And then? Strain them through a hair sieve. What in the world was a hair sieve?

And the person who took this drink would find anything that was lost. Madness. But what if it worked? If he was quick, he could be there even ahead of Chris. On the last stretch Alec began to run hard.

"Grandpa!"

"How late you are today, my boy."

"I was with Chris. I found a house, Grandpa. It really is in the middle of the woods. A long way off."

"Oh. Come and eat quickly, or everything will be cold."

The garden lettuce was already on the table with an egg from Grandpa's hens. The potatoes were still frying in the pan.

"Grandpa, come and see what I've got."

Grandpa had to put his glasses on first. He did not understand.

"Gray threads, Grandpa. You know. The threads in the book."

"Oh, quite."

"Do you believe it, Grandpa? Do you think it's possible, that you can find what you have lost?"

"If it's in the book, yes," said Grandpa. "It's very strange, of course, but there are so many wonderful things in it. You will see that it is true."

"Shall we try it?"

"What do you mean? Try what?"

"Cook the fungus and then— Grandpa, what's a hair sieve?"

"What are you talking about now?"

"You'll have to read it through again," said Alec. "Have we a glazed earthenware pan?"

Grandpa shook his head and said no more. After the meal he went to wash the dishes as usual, and when everything was cleared away, he said, "Now we'll go and have another look. Get the book out of the cupboard."

At last. Grandpa read it out slowly.

"A hair sieve is a strainer. So what you think is that this is the 'friend'—these threads you have found. It is possible. It will have to be tested."

"Shall we do it? Shall I get some rainwater from the barrel? What shall I put the toadstools in?"

Grandpa allowed his glasses to slip down to the point of his nose, and he looked at Alec. "What did you say?"

"What shall I put them in?"

"You said 'toadstools.'"

"Yes, they're a kind of fungus. You can't see it so well anymore now, but there was a real little hat on top."

"I'm naturally not going to cook any toadstools I don't know."

"Oh."

"They might easily be poisonous."

"Of course they're not. It wouldn't have been in the book then, would it?"

"I don't know what is in the book. I can only read the translation. Cook the fungus and drink it up. No, Alec, it won't do."

Alec very much wanted to say, "Why didn't you say so sooner?" But he never said that kind of thing to his grandfather. He was silent.

"You might as well throw them out right away," said Grandpa, "and then go and wash your hands thoroughly."

Alec did as he was told.

"It's a good thing we're not really missing anything," Grandpa comforted him, "or have you actually lost something?"

"No, Grandpa, nothing." And he thought to himself, Oh, well, it's probably all nonsense anyway.

Chris walked thoughtfully toward Janna's house, the piece of moss with the toadstools on it held loosely in his hand. He had them. Would he at last be able to do something more real than shelling beans? Or not?

He could not use them until Janna had gone. His plan to be ahead of her had therefore failed already, except of course if she were wrong and found nothing tonight.

Chris thought he was gradually gaining some understanding of how magic worked. There was probably some poison or other in the rottentooth that made your memory work differently, so that memories of events that had escaped your attention came to the surface. You would become rather sleepy, and then suddenly you would know: I was sitting here when I used my penknife for the last time, that's where I put my diary down, that's who borrowed my book. But if he were to find the treasure of an old baron who was long dead, whom he had never known, it might not help at all even if he cooked fungus by the pound. He would get nothing but a headache.

Too bad. He must go and see Alec tomorrow and find out if there was anything that could be of more use to him.

Chris was walking more and more slowly. What was he to do with the fungus? Not throw it away, that was sure. He walked behind the barn. Here and there you could look between the planks and the roof thatch. Somewhere up there he could keep the bundle of moss nice and dry. There was moss growing there already.

What was scrabbling in there? The cats? Or was it a wild animal? A polecat. With great care he hid the rottentooth that he might never use and then walked around the barn and opened the door. Not a polecat, Janna.

"Ah, you're there, are you? High time. You can come and give me a hand. What do you think? What else do we need?"

There were all kinds of tools, rusty, but still good: spades and rakes, pickaxes, hatchets large and small, and a carpenter's chest too. Janna had already laid out one shovel and one pickaxe.

"A crowbar would do no harm either," she said. "It may easily be packed in a strong chest."

"Twenty years in the ground," said Chris. "A chest wouldn't be too strong after that."

"Perhaps it's not in the ground."

"But you've put a shovel out already, Janna. I thought you knew exactly where it was."

"I know and I don't know. I know the place he chose, but William would never dig a hole himself and he wouldn't let anyone else do it either. Then they would know where he was hiding his money."

"He could have asked the gardener to dig a hole for a tree and put a chest in it when the gardener had gone."

"A tree. . . ." Janna picked up one of the hatchets. "No," she said then, "the gardener would have noticed." And she replaced the hatchet.

"You had better go and get the milk cart, Chris. There's plenty of room in it, and we will eat before we go."

"What time are you going, Janna? Does it have to be quite dark?"

"Nine o'clock, there at nine-thirty. Then we shall still be able to see when we arrive. You must come too, of course."

"Oh."

"Did you think I could carry all that money alone? William was as rich as rich. And if the heir is as shabby as you say, there must be a great deal hidden."

"But Janna, you can't take it away just like that!"

"*I* can't, but with the milk cart we shall manage all right together."

The milk cart was a wooden box on wheels that she moved milk churns and buckets about with.

"I mean," said Chris, "the money isn't yours. What are you going to do with it?"

Janna began to laugh in her own peculiar way. "When I have it, it's mine. I only want to have it. But I'm not going to do anything with it."

Chris went off to fetch the milk cart. He had to think it over again. Of course it would be very exciting, and fun, but it was downright theft. He could not be a party to that.

CHAPTER XVIII

The Rose Garden

The Hazelhurst house had never been very lively. When it was still inhabited, there were thick carpets everywhere, over which the residents moved with dignity. Their voices were low and courteous. Children. had to behave themselves, and servants were not heard at all.

The bell by the tall front door had a resonant peal, but it was scarcely ever rung. And there was a row of little bells by the kitchen door too. Beside each one was a tag with a number on it that tipped up at the slightest movement. That way you could tell in which room the bell was being rung.

Now William Vandyck had moved into Hazelhurst Castle with his friends. The wooden floors and stairs echoed with their heavy footsteps, and the window-panes shook with their voices.

"William, how do you get this pump going?"

"Where shall I put this gas stove down?"

"Do you know how many potatoes to cook for eight people?"

"You don't have to cook any potatoes at all for eight people. Much too much work. Use spaghetti."

"We haven't any."

"Bo! Bo! Would you mind going in to the village again? We need spaghetti."

The rumpus went on in the poor, bare house until half-past eight. Then a steaming pan of spaghetti was carried out to the rose garden. And plates. And spoons. Some of them brought chairs. Others brought a rug to sit on. Glasses, but not for everyone.

"Now is there anything else we need?"

"Salt. Where is the salt?"

"Already in the spaghetti."

"It may need a little more."

"Isn't it too cold to sit out here?"

"Not at all."

But it really was cold. A mist was rising from the back garden. Then Louis and Barbara brought dead branches from the elder tree and the rhododendrons, and William fetched a newspaper. There was a big slab of cement among the roses. No one could figure out what it had been used for, but it was just what they needed. With the paper and a fine pyramid of kindling, he built up a warm fire. They leaned comfortably against each other and pushed the empty pans and plates to one side.

"What a lovely garden, William."

"And a really beautiful house. What an absolute shame

that no one's lived in it for so long. Why did your family leave it empty?"

William sighed.

"Of course it's none of our business," said Greta.

"Of course not," said Tim. "We are only here to find William's inheritance, not to stick our noses into his family affairs. Can't you grasp the fine distinction?"

William sighed again. They thought him too mysterious. Perhaps they were right. He could hear his mother's voice again, "You don't talk about that. One doesn't do that kind of thing." There was always such an awful lot that "one didn't do." "Uncle William was a little difficult" and "Everyone has his little ways." The little ways of Uncle William must have been quite alarming, but she was so scared of talking about them that he himself knew regrettably little.

"I wouldn't mind telling you everything," he said, "because everyone who had anything to do with the matter is dead, but I have already told you all I know. My uncle was the only son. My grandparents were here for the better part of the year, but they had another house in The Hague and when they were old they stayed there. Uncle William always lived here. I believe he lived quite simply. He never allowed anything in the house to be changed or modernized. And I don't get the impression that he handed out much money in other ways or was extravagant, but I don't know for sure."

He hesitated for a moment. "Indecent remarks," his Aunt Reine had written. That didn't make you poor.

Indecent *acts* certainly could cost a lot of money. Oh, well, she had been a good deal stuffier than his mother. It probably meant nothing.

"He was simply a little bit crazy. I know that he sold off the farms that belonged to the estate one by one and also that he had a collection of old coins, but it's only because of Aunt Reine's letter that I know they may still be here. I thought they were sold by now, to pay estate duties or something. Uncle William was taken to an institution about twenty years ago and died there three years later. Something must have happened, of course, some reason why after all those years he was locked away, but I was only ten at that time.

"No one was ever able or willing to tell me what happened. I was already trying to find a buyer when I found the message: your Uncle William's coin collection is probably in or near Hazelhurst Castle, and it must not fall into the wrong hands.

"Why did she never go and look for herself? She could have sent me here. Perhaps she was a bit crazy too. It's quite likely. And here I find the same secretiveness: the farmer, the old girl who kept house, the gardener's family. They know something, that's clear, but it doesn't come out. Oh, well, I'll sell the lot. I need all the money I can get for it to pay the tax."

"You can't do that, William."

"I can, damn it. That's the way it is!" William angrily kicked a burning piece of wood back to the fire with the side of his shoe. Saskia began to laugh.

"We can see you're getting too big for your boots! What size do you take?"

"Size fifteen, extra wide."

"Don't sell it, William," said Guy. "You *need* a castle. I don't know a single ordinary house that has room for a closet to put *your* shoes in. We'll help you. We'll stay here until the coins have been found."

"And the mystery solved," said Bo, "the mystery of the uncle."

He began to sing:

> "Uncle, where is your gold?
> *Where* can Uncle's gold be?
> Under the old oak tree
> Or is it sold?
> I would I could it hold—

No, that won't do. Help me, Tim."

"It rolled," said Tim.

"Oh, Uncle," Bo began again. He often made up songs when there was a party or one of their friends was going to be married. He did it best when there were some girls with them and they were in an after-a-good-dinner mood, as they were now. The girls sang along with him, drawing the notes out.

> "Oh, Uncle, wheeeere is your gold?
> Wheeeeere can Uncle's gold be?
> Under the old oak tree

Or is it sold?
I had a dream of old
that Uncle's gold had rolled
right down the path to me.
Where caaaan that rolled gold be?"

Their voices sounded clearly through the still evening. Slot's dog began to join in. The song of Uncle's gold could even be heard from the cottages. And, of course, it was easy to hear every word behind the wall, where Janna and Chris had stopped with their milk cart full of digging tools.

Janna was leaning against the wall, as cross as two sticks. Chris climbed onto the cart to look over the wall. He could have done so at the gap, but then they might have seen him. Here he was hidden by a hazelnut tree.

"There are a lot of them, Janna, eight I think. Yes, eight."

"If you want to turn over a whole wood with eight people, it will take a few days."

"It doesn't look as if they were going off to dig at once."

"They will get tired and cold. We'll wait till they're asleep, and then we'll go to it, hee-hee-hee."

"They're not going to be tired, or cold either, for a long time. They've got a fire."

The smell of burning wood wafted over the wall; the heat did not. Chris gazed longingly at the flames. He was cold already. And the prospect of spending hours here with Janna while William and his friends had fun over there seemed very disagreeable. But he had better not say anything. Janna was not going to give up her plan for his sake.

He jumped to the ground, right onto a twig, which snapped. The group by the fire heard nothing. They were singing.

"We must do something about it," said Janna. "I'll take care of the rats. Will you do the ants?"

"Ants? I? What am I supposed to do?"

"Close to the rose garden there is a nest of red ants. They would very much enjoy cleaning up the dishes and the pans. You must take care of it. They would also enjoy creeping into clothes and biting warm human flesh."

Chris knew now what Janna meant. He had certainly been able to affect people and animals with the magic stone.

"I can't. I'm not allowed to use the stone."

"I know for sure that you can do it without the stone," said Janna. "It will be good practice. Or would you rather do the rats?"

"Rats? No. I'll find out if I can do it with ants."

He sat down against the wall beside Janna, completely relaxed, and began to think about ants. What would it feel like to be an ant? A small, shiny body with busy little legs. What would you see from those bulging, faceted eyes? Could an ant smell? Or did they smell together? They always worked with each other. Each one carried a portion of a fly.

There they came, in a narrow, wiggling line, the red army on the move toward the spaghetti pan. One after another, they crawled along the handle, on their way to the sticky remnants of the food. With busy jaws they nibbled at the plates; one or two were already struggling in the tomato sauce. Greta noticed a bite, Guy felt a tickling in his jeans, Louis jumped to his feet.

"Oh, look, how sweet," said Barbara, "a mouse."

A young rat was sitting on its haunches, staring at her.

"That's not a mouse," said William. "It's a rat."

"I still think he's sweet. Hi, rattypie. What's your name? Come and see your little friend. Do you like cheese?"

"Rats and ants," said William glumly. "In the old days a nightingale used to sing here."

"Really? Let's sit still for a while. Perhaps it will come back."

"I can't sit still. The ants are eating the flesh off my bottom. My left leg has already come unstuck."

"You're putting it on. Just a few miserable ants."

"Formic acid from ant stings is good for you. Didn't you know that? If you let them bite you, you'll never get rheumatism."

"Guy, don't be so wild. You've made my rat run away."

"There are more of them. Take a look."

"I'm leaving." Saskia felt threatened by just one ant, one mosquito, one spider, one baby mouse.

"I'm going too," said Tim. He was not much braver. "William, there are no rats in your castle, are there?"

"Never noticed," said William.

"As long as you don't leave any food about," said Louis. "We should have cleared up here first. Now they won't go away. We'd better break it up. I'm going to put up my tent."

"How do you dare, with all these monsters about?"

"Animals are never aggressive without reason. When I was camping in Canada I found bear tracks around the tent next morning."

"How super!" said Barbara. Saskia shuddered. All the others had an opinion somewhere between the two. Their unity was broken. They could not sing together any longer now. They did clear up together, however.

"Can we leave the fire like that?"

"I'll keep an eye on it," said Louis. "I'll leave the tent open, and we won't be going to sleep right away."

When everyone had gone in and Greta had already crept into her sleeping bag in the tent, he walked about, swept the ashes together, and looked around to see if everything was in order. But he did not see Janna's glittering eyes under the hazelnut tree. Now she was standing on the cart. She saw Louis going into the tent, close to the fire, which was still glowing, very close to the place where she wanted to dig. She could clearly hear talk and laughter. It was impossible to do anything there tonight.

She stepped down and gave Chris a nudge. He was leaning sleepily against the wall, not feeling the cold and hearing nothing. He was still an ant. He saw pine needles like fence posts and grains of sand like blocks of stone, but he could climb over them lightly and easily and he found a piece of spaghetti as thick as a truck tire. Someone was tugging at it. Another ant? No, Janna.

"Come on, we have to go. Get up."

Deep sigh. "Are we going to dig?"

"No, we're not going to dig. Another time. Or never. I shall . . . I shall think of something. You can be sure I shall think of something. Come on."

Chris rose to his feet with difficulty. He had the feeling that he must first make hands and feet grow on his thin little legs. "Didn't it work, Janna? I thought it went all right."

He was coming to a little and was going to climb on the cart to have a look. But she tugged at his arm. "We're going home. Didn't you hear me?"

Together they pulled the cart to the path. If only a human being were as strong as an ant!

Janna said nothing. She was very angry and walked along muttering to herself. Only when they were nearly home did Chris learn that a tent had been put up close to the place where she thought old William's treasure was hidden.

"I can't go there by day, and if someone is sleeping there in the tent, I can't go at night either."

"But why don't you send some rats and ants into the tent?"

"It doesn't work. I can't do it with the man in the tent. He knows animals. But I'll think of something. You wait. . . ."

CHAPTER XIX

Abracadabra

Chris could not get to sleep. He was still completely under the influence of his evening's experience. He thought that he now knew more about ants than anyone who had read ten books about them, more than he could have learned by looking at them for a week. Or perhaps doing that could give you the antlike feeling too. He should be able to do the same with cats, birds, trees. He had made magic! He had not used the magic stone, and yet it had worked.

He was with Janna to learn everything she knew about the powers in nature. He had thought up to now that it was going very slowly. But today he had taken a leap forward. Had he learned so much from her without noticing, or did the stone make him more sensitive, even if he was not holding it? He was not allowed to use it for one year. Perhaps what he had done today was wrong. He did not really know for sure whether he had sent the ants to the people beside the fire. Quite likely the ants had found the way themselves, attracted by the smell of the food. He would never know for sure.

How angry Janna had been when it hadn't helped! A real wicked witch. Chris understood the dangers of magic very well. People who could cast spells generally got their own way. They grew angry more quickly than anyone if anything went wrong. He was curious to know what she would think of now. He would prefer to have nothing at all to do with it. He must leave early in the morning. Then she would not be able to bring him into her affairs. Yes, that was the best idea. Before Janna had time to send him to do anything, he would go to see Alec.

When Chris reached this point in his thinking, he fell asleep peacefully enough, and he woke up at exactly the time he had planned.

The little room where he slept lay on the west side of the house. The sun never shone into it in the morning, but he could hear from the peaceful clucking of the hens that it was going to be a fine day. Janna had no shower in her house. If the weather was bad, he had to wash in the kitchen. Otherwise, he did so outside by the well. That was better. He could splash in all directions and make a mess, and the pigeons sat on the roof of the well, looking on.

When he went out, Janna was already stirring a pot. Every day she made a big pancake for breakfast, and she gave the larger part to Chris. It smelled deliciously of fried butter. It always put him in a good mood at once and today more than ever. All week he had stayed nervously at home, but he was not going to be ordered about any-more. Plop, puss, out of the way! Or do you want a bath too? He splashed harder than usual. Today he was going to do what *he* wanted. Surely he was just as good a witch as Janna! Was she still as angry as before?

When he came back to the kitchen, she was standing with her back to him, an improbably large pancake turner in her hand. The mixture in the pan moved as if it were alive, making soft, sputtering sounds.

Janna said, "Chris, you must go and see that friend of yours again today. I've got a couple of things to do, and I would rather be alone for them."

At once Chris felt a tremendous curiosity arising in him, but all he said was, "Sure."

"And you might just as well throw away that moss you hid under the roof of the barn. It's no good any longer."

"That's what I thought."

Perhaps Janna was the better witch of the two, after all.

Immediately after breakfast he set out. As soon as he was into the woods he put his mind to thinking about Alec's magic book. Now he was going to see it at last. Alec's grandfather had promised. If only there was some-thing usable in it. There *must* be something in it that he could use.

Alec and Grandpa were still at breakfast when the front doorbell rang.

"Hello, Chris. You're up early!"

"Yes," said Chris. "I thought perhaps we could go and do something nice today."

"That's good," said Grandpa. "There is still that bird-house in the shed, Alec. If Chris is good with his hands, you could repair it together."

"Oh, no," said Alec, "not when the weather is so nice. I'd rather go into the woods today."

"If you'll let me, I would very much like to have a look at the old book, Mr. Aulder."

"Oh, yes, that's true. You're the boy who is so interested in it. That's nice, yes."

"Shall I get it, Grandpa?"

"In a minute. Not so fast. Clear away first."

Alec was not allowed to go to the cupboard until the last crumb had been swept off the table. Grandpa was nervous and fussy. He was not pleased that Chris should see where the key hung. But at last they had done it. The little chest was on the table.

Chris was, if possible, even more disappointed than Alec the first time. He couldn't read anything either, of course. He was actually allowed to hold the little book written by the grandfather in 1761 for a minute, but it was about anything but magic. The schoolmaster had written out a vocabulary and some notes on language, but they were no use either, unless you had time to study them for days or weeks. Alec stood looking on, a little bored. He preferred to be out of doors. Chris asked if Grandpa would tell them something about it, but Grandpa would not come to the point.

Then Alec said suddenly, "Grandpa, I thought there was much more inside the little chest."

"Yes," said Grandpa. "You see, it's like this. This is not actually the genuine Auldland book. The real one is so old that it falls to pieces if you touch it. But when it was in better condition, someone copied it out word for word. When that copy begins to wear out, it has to be done again. The fragments that are left of the oldest book of all I have stored in another place."

"But the book Chris has there is not the same as the one I looked at last time either. It's like it, but it's different."

"It's by the same man. I have taken the other one out too. With hindsight, I did think it was a little bit dangerous for you to have it."

"What could be dangerous about a little book like that?"

"Well, you were going to eat toadstools, weren't you? But very well. If I am here, I don't mind Chris seeing it."

Grandpa took his key ring out of his pocket and went back to the big cupboard. He tried a key, which fitted one of the big drawers, and turned it twice. Under a pile of cloths lay the stiff brown book, with more papers and some green writing.

"I used to think it didn't mean anything," said Grandpa. "Powers did not mean much to me, but once I tried something out and then I really did get a fright."

"What did you do?"

"There's something in it about how to make rain. And the garden was so dry." Grandpa began to laugh. "I didn't believe it, of course. I did it for a joke. There was a terrible storm."

Alec looked disbelieving.

Chris said, "But that was a good thing, wasn't it? Or was it much too violent? Was the garden spoiled?"

"It was just the kind of shower my little garden needed."

"It probably just happened to rain by accident," said Alec.

"That's it," said Grandpa, "and by coincidence it was dry again a few weeks later."

"Oh," said Chris breathlessly, "and you did it again and it worked again. You're a real rainmaker."

"Storm maker," said Grandpa, "and now I'm sure you understand why I keep that book under lock and key. Not everything in it is equally clear. You might unleash dangerous powers."

He stood by the table, the thick pages flicking one after another through his hands.

"Shall we go out?" asked Alec. He thought Grandpa was being silly. It didn't matter, it was his own grandpa, but Chris shouldn't be involved.

"I was going to be allowed to see it," said Chris. Oh, please, he thought, this is it. This is the whole thing, and in a minute he'll be shutting everything up again, and I don't know what. If only I could do something, like moving the ants. But he knew that took time. You had to let yourself go completely to do it. At present he was full of tension.

"Oh," said Grandpa, "it's nonsense, of course. Look, it says here, for instance, how you can call up a spirit. You have to stand between five oaks and blow the number three on a ram's horn. What does that mean, blow the number three? Well, suppose it works and the spirit comes. You wouldn't be able to see it in any case. You have to remember that I'm an old man. I have not much to do, and an old family heirloom like this interests me. I have worked out all the things in this writing that I can understand. But most of it is . . . abracadabra. Ha ha ha."

He was already beginning to pack the papers up again, putting everything in the chest from habit, but he remembered in time. The brown book and the green writing disappeared at the bottom of the drawer.

"Forget about it," said Grandpa. "That business about the storm was a joke of course. But you can have another look, with pleasure."

"Thank you," said Chris, "but I do believe it."

"Do come along now," said Alec. Chris was fine as long as he didn't go crazy along with Grandpa.

CHAPTER XX

Ram's Horn

When they were outside and walking in the familiar direction of the castle, Alec asked, "How did it go? Did Janna find the treasure last night?"

Chris told him how they had marched through the woods together with the milk cart, how they had sat waiting for hours behind the wall, and how it had all been for nothing because two of William's guests had camped in the garden. He left the rats and ants out of the story.

"But now I know that Janna wanted to search in the garden."

"Shall we go there?"

"We could."

"If there is nobody at home, I would like to go into the garden and have a look around."

"But William himself did that long ago."

"Yes, that's true. I wish I knew what your Janna knows. But can we find out what it is?"

"Never," said Chris decidedly.

"What did you do with the gray threads?"

"Nothing. They're no good anymore."

"Why did you call them rottentooth?"

"Just did. That's what Janna calls them."

"You believe the things in Grandpa's book, don't you?"

"Sometimes," said Chris cautiously.

"The appearance is deceptive, yet the powers of which we are not aware form the real world."

"How did you get hold of that?"

"It was in the book. I was thinking of it all the way home yesterday. If it is true, I don't care for it. It means you can't believe what you see."

"All you have to believe is that there is more than you see."

"Like a spirit that comes when you blow the number three?"

"For instance. I know what that means: blowing the number three."

"I know where there's a ram's horn." Alec thought, Let Chris blow. Then he'll see that no spirit comes. They don't exist. I don't want them to exist.

Chris thought, You need more than a ram's horn and five oak trees. The description is not complete. Nothing will come of it, so it can't do any harm if I do it, because it's only a game. He did not think, I'm not allowed to do magic for a year. Never play with powers you don't know, because you can't foresee the consequences. Grandpa thought it was dangerous for us to read the book. Deep down he knew these things quite well, of course. It was really exciting.

"Where's this ram's horn?"

"On the Rengerink farm. He's a farmer I've helped from time to time. He keeps sheep, and there are about six horns on the pasture fence."

"Would you be allowed to have one?"

"I'll ask. We'll have to turn back, though. He lives on the path that goes to the right past Grandpa's cottage. But perhaps we can reach it by way of the woods as well. His house is close to the other side of the woods."

"Let's go on then. We can look out for a place where there are five oak trees."

"There must be a thousand oak trees in the woods."

"I think it would work better if they were exactly the same distance from each other."

"Otherwise, I suppose we'd get a spirit with one short arm?"

"No, nothing that you'd be able to see. A spirit that can't say its *r*'s."

"Oh, yes, then we'll ask it, 'Spirit, where is the treasure?' And it will say, 'The bawon buwied it.' "

"Where did the bawon buwy the tweasure?"

"In the cemetewy natuwally, under a gwavestone."

"Under which gwavestone?"

"The one that has witten on it in big letters: 'Here lies Wengewink.' "

"Or Woterdink."

"I can hear those wetched dogs alweady."

They had reached Hazelhurst Castle, and they could hear the chatter and laughter of William and his friends as well as the dogs. Some of them had just woken up, most were having breakfast, and Louis pulled the sleeping bags out of his tent while he sang at the top of his voice, "Uncle, where is your gold?"

"Yes," said Chris, "I'm sure he wants to know, but we shall find the treasure, because we have a spirit to help."

"First blow the number three," said Alec. "You said you knew how to do that, but I don't understand it."

"It just means a third, of course."

"Oh." Alec did know what a third was, but he was not sure it was so easy to blow it on a ram's horn.

That was no problem for Chris. "I've been taking trumpet lessons for a year or two. You just get hold of the hooter, and I'll look after the third. Taraa!" He blew between his hands, and the sound really was quite trumpet-like, but Alec didn't believe that it would make a ghost appear.

The way along the edge of the woods was long and hot. They walked past meadows and fields of corn, sometimes over a high ridge and at other times through a ditch overgrown with brambles. But the woods were so thick that they couldn't find a place to enter to look for the five oak trees.

The Rengerink farm lay silently in the sunshine, the yard freshly swept. The farm dog wandered lazily up to them. He barked, because it was his duty, without much enthusiasm. When Alec and Chris walked toward the house, he trudged peacefully behind them. The little curtain at the kitchen window moved to one side, and they saw a face.

"I was afraid there was no one there," said Alec. "It's all so quiet."

They knocked at the kitchen door and walked straight in. Inside, the kitchen was cool and dark. Henry's wife was peeling potatoes, and a big piece of meat lay sputtering in the frying pan.

"Isn't Henry home?" asked Alec.

"He'll be coming in to eat in half an hour. You can wait if you like."

"Thanks. We'll just walk around for a bit."

She nodded and dropped a big potato into a pan.

"I'd rather ask Henry himself," said Alec. "He's very friendly."

The hedge around the garden was freshly trimmed, the beds of mignonette and petunias were weeded, and the standard roses tied up. Fuchsias with their little red bells were growing in big pots.

"Look," said Alec, "there are the horns I saw."

They were nailed firmly to a wooden plank fence and obviously served as decoration.

"They won't want to lose those," said Chris. "Everything is so terribly neat and tidy here, and they keep it that way just for themselves, because no one ever passes. The road stops here."

Past the biggest barn a narrow path led into the woods. That too was smooth and clean, but grass grew under the trees, and when they followed the path, they could see that it was never used. Young birch trees were already growing between the old cart tracks.

"We must ask where it leads. Perhaps we can go back this way."

"We could go and look for the oak trees now."

They did not find any and turned back when they heard the sound of a tractor. That might be Henry. And so it was. He raised a hand in greeting, because you could hear nothing over the roar of the engine. Chris thought he looked rather surly, but he got a pleasant surprise.

"A ram's horn? What do you want to do with it? Trumpet? Ha ha ha. Well, just you take one and do your tooting some way off."

Alec was modestly going to take the smallest, but the farmer said, "If you're going to do it, you must do it properly. Here, take this one." And he pulled off the biggest of all, from the middle of the row. "They're just hanging here. They're no use to anyone."

"Henry, where does that little path lead?"

"Around the back of Hazelhurst Castle. We haven't been that way for years. It's from the old days. My father used to work in the garden there. Wouldn't you like something to eat, boys? It must be nearly twelve o'clock."

"As late as that?" said Alec, startled. "Grandpa is expecting me back at half past. I can't stay, because it will make me later still."

Henry had a telephone. They could not get out of it, so they ate with the Rengerink family: potatoes, buttermilk, meat with a rim of fat round it, and stewed pears. There was a great deal, although no one had expected the two boys to be there.

When they were ready to go, Henry said, "Alec, I've got the turnips up, but when we go and dig the potatoes, you can come along. You'll get just as black."

"Thank you. Thank you very much." And they were off. They had eaten too much and too early, and the day was very warm. They walked and walked among spruce firs and birch trees, under an old beech, but they didn't see a single oak. Chris scratched with his penknife at the ram's horn, and now and then he blew a few notes on it to see if it sounded like anything.

They sat down for a short rest, and it did sound like something. But it could be better, Chris thought, and he went on scratching away at it. They got up and walked.

"We must be quite close to Hazelhurst Castle now. We've been walking a long time."

They pulled off their shirts and flapped them to keep off the insects that were trying to settle on their bare backs. They walked, and they saw two oak trees.

"Perhaps we've missed a fork in the path."

They walked and walked, until "Look!"

"Oh, yes, there are five of them."

"It will have to be here then. We don't have to sit right in the middle. That's where the sun is shining."

"Yes, right in the middle."

"I don't believe spirits like too much light. And in any case I want to rest a bit first. Oh, am I thirsty!"

They slumped onto the ground beside the sturdiest oak. Both of them were very thirsty indeed.

CHAPTER XXI

The Wifie

The dark oak trees gave the place an atmosphere of solemnity, but the boys didn't really notice in the excitement of finding the particular spot they had been looking for so long. It was quite silent here. Only the faint twitter of birds came from a long way off.

"I don't believe we've walked any farther than this morning," said Chris. "It only feels like it because of the heat and because we're a bit tired and so full from lunch."

"Yes," said Alec, "that's what I think too. They should have planted some bilberries or raspberries here."

"But they didn't."

"Well, if you blow a spirit up out of your hooter, ask it for water first, before asking where the treasure is."

"All right. Shall we try it?"

"Okay."

In the center of the group of trees, the ground was a

little lower. A yellow grass grew there, and it tickled high up on their legs. Chris gave a couple of deep sighs. They were behaving now as if it were all nonsense, but he was really very keen for something to happen. Not a spirit in the form of a white cloud, like the story books, but *something*. He was going to put all his power into it. Another sigh.

"Toot, tooot, tooot!" A breeze rustled through the grass. Very good. It might start like that. Once more.

"Toot, tooot, tooot!"

"It does sound real," whispered Alec.

"Quiet." Two more deep breaths. Perhaps it had to be done five times, or seven times, Chris thought. But he did not blow anymore. Someone was coming. A man—Tom.

"Hello!"

They had been eating with him, and he had not spoken a word. Now he said in his indistinct voice, "He does it quite well. Can I have a try?"

Could he have walked behind them all the way without their noticing anything? Chris asked him, but Tom either could not or would not answer. He was only interested in the ram's horn. "I found it," he said.

"And I made it," said Chris. "If you want one I'll make another." But he was thinking, You're not having this one. "It's very difficult to blow on it. I can do it because I've had trumpet lessons. I'll be happy to make you one that is easier to blow."

That went over Tom's head. "I found it."

Alec suddenly noticed that he had a big bottle in his

pocket. "Tom, have you got something to drink there?"

"Water." They were each given a swallow from the bottle. Then he began again, "Please, can I have the horn back? I found it." And Henry had given it away. This was a problem.

"It's broken," said Chris. "Look here. The point is missing."

"I want the horn. Then I'll show you the wifie."

"What did you say?"

"The wifie is over there."

"Tom, shouldn't you go home? You're supposed to help Henry. They'll be eating soon." Alec mentioned everything he could think of to get rid of the man. But Tom did not go.

"A big, fat wifie," he said dreamily. And then again, "I want the horn back."

"Okay," said Chris. "Tom, I'd like to see the wifie. You just show us the way."

"Over there." Tom was going in the direction where there was no path, straight through the trees. He looked back now and again to see if they were following. Alec was afraid they were going to get lost, and he thought, The woods come to an end somewhere, because it's not as big as the world, but if you walk in a circle there is no end. And they were not walking straight ahead, because the trees and bushes grew irregularly. It looked as if Tom knew where he was going, but how far could you trust a man like that?

"Let's go back, Chris. This is no good."

"No," said Chris. "I want to see the wifie."

"On we go then." Alec was just as thirsty as before by now.

They walked a long way. Alec and Chris put on their shirts again, because having a branch whip back against your bare body is no fun. Tom in his clogs strode ahead. Sometimes he seemed not quite certain what he was doing, until they came to a crooked pine or a tall maple that he apparently recognized. At last they reached a fallen tree, thickly overgrown with ivy.

"There," said Tom. "The fat wifie."

Chris and Alec climbed over the tree. Tom was right. There was a big, fat wifie. She was made of gray cement, and the biggest thing about her was the bulging bottom on which she sat. In front she had two enormous bulges from which you could see that it was a woman. Her arms were pinned to her sides, and her legs were monstrously fat and far too short for their width. She was in the shape of a pyramid. A broad, flat head was set directly on the body, with no neck. The point of her nose had been broken off, and you could see that she had been completely overgrown with ivy and moss, which had been carefully removed. The whole thing was at least six feet high.

Tom walked around it.

"Beautiful wifie," said Tom, patting the yard-wide buttocks.

"That's okay," said Alec, gazing with revulsion at the colossus.

And Chris said, "So this is it, William's treasure, and we are the first there."

"The treasure?" Alec began to grin, for he suddenly understood. "Do you think it's here . . . oh yes, is that what you think, Chris?"

"The treasure is in here, for sure," said Chris. He too began to walk around the wifie. She had burst open here and there, but not enough for him to see inside. He could see that the cement had been plastered on wire netting, because rusty ends were sticking out. Chris gave it a push, but there was no movement. It must be as heavy as lead.

"How did they get it here?" Alec wondered. "And why?"

"Because of this," said Chris, pointing to the front, where it was so obvious that the cement structure represented a woman.

Tom grinned. "Beautiful wifie," he said, and stroked one of the mighty thighs.

"That's true, Tom. Thank you for bringing us here," said Chris. "Here." He gave Tom the ram's horn. The man clutched it greedily and made a move to go, but thought better of it.

"She's my wifie," said Tom, looking angry and threatening. They were not to think that they had bought her for his own ram's horn. He had simply wanted to show the statue off with pride, and now, suddenly realizing this meant that she was no longer his alone, he regretted it.

Alec had been just about to try a hard knock against a spot where there were a lot of brown spikes, to see if something was really hidden inside the heavy mass. But he preferred not to have a fight with such a strong, simple man.

"You'll take us back, won't you, Tom?" asked Chris. "We can't find the way on our own."

The dark face cleared at once. In the big, confusing world, where there was so much he did not understand, Tom always excelled in one thing. He could find his way home, wherever he was, like a carrier pigeon, and he showed off his skill as often as he had the chance. First he pointed once more to the wifie. "Not talk about it. You hear?"

"Yes. Yes."

"Come along then."

And they thrust their way back through the wilderness. As a precaution Alec broke a twig off a bush from time to time. He hoped this would help him to find the way another time—preferably today—without a guide. Chris began to tell a dirty joke that he had just remembered.

They reached the grove with the five oak trees, and there Tom took the ram's horn out of his pocket.

"No," said Chris, "not here. You must try somewhere else."

He took it over to the path. Tom blew, without success. "I told you it was difficult." Chris showed him how. After five more efforts, a little squeak came out. Now Tom wanted to return to the place where he had found Alec and Chris, and once again Chris persuaded him not too.

"Take us a little farther, Tom. Are we near Hazelhurst Castle yet?"

Alec said, "I suppose you're scared that Tom might call up a ghost."

Chris treated the matter as a joke. In his view the summoning of the spirit had been completely successful. After all, they had had exactly what they wished for, even the water that Alec had been longing for. The most practical way a spirit could provide them with that was through someone with a bottle. Someone like Tom, whose own mind was a little weak. Oh, yes, as far as Chris was concerned the experiment had been a splendid success. But he did not know what might happen if the spell were used by a primitive man who had little power over his feelings. And he knew quite well that he should not express these thoughts to Alec.

CHAPTER XXII

William

When they were rid of Tom and his horn, Alec's and Chris's first thought was once again: water. Under the trees was all right, but the way to Slot's farm was burning hot. They decided to go to the cottages in spite of the notice: *No Admission to Unauthorized Persons.* And fortunately no one forbade them to drink from the tap. They poured water over their faces and hair and rinsed out their sweaty shirts. They put them on again, soaking wet, and then they were ready for a little conference. They walked around to the back of the castle. Chris took a quick look through the gap in the wall. Far away, in the high grass on the other side of the rose garden and on the terrace, a few people were sunbathing. They must think it was too hot to go treasure hunting today. In the shade the stone wall was beautifully cool to lean against. They chose the same place under the hazel tree where Chris had waited with Janna.

"I wonder who that money really belongs to," said Alec. "Our villain was looking for it, but if it were his he would surely know where to find it."

"It was his uncle's," said Chris.

"Yes, and he's been dead twenty years. He hid it, so he didn't want the family to have it."

"He was crazy."

"Yes."

"Do you want to keep it yourself?"

"I would want to know all kinds of things first. For instance: how long do you have to wait before something lost stops belonging to anyone? And if you find something, who has a right to it? It might be Tom. Actually I would much rather Tom had it than that fellow with the yellow bike."

"Perhaps the owner of the land has a right to it when it doesn't belong to anyone else. And that would also be the fellow with the yellow bike."

"Do you want him to have it?"

"I don't know. I think you're right. We have to know all those things first. And we have to know what it is. We haven't seen any money yet."

"You can count on it. It's in there." Alec began to laugh. He could see the wifie before his eyes. "He certainly was good and crazy, that uncle, that's for sure. Crazy about women, I think."

"Yes." Chris nodded thoughtfully. "But who can we ask? No chance with Janna. Your grandpa?" He stopped. Had he heard something?

"Grandpa doesn't know," said Alec.

"Quiet."

Something cracked behind the wall. Was someone walking there? Yes. Two young men were climbing fast over the crumbling stones. In two strides they were standing beside Alec and Chris.

"Tell us."

"You can tell us everything."

Alec and Chris were silent.

"You have found something. What is it?"

"It's quite all right to talk about it. We heard everything."

The boys simply looked at one another.

"Perhaps you'd rather tell William, the owner."

"Want a glass of lemonade? Come inside a minute, er, outside, and—"

"Come on, Alec, let's go and talk somewhere else. Somewhere where we won't be spied on."

Tim had heard them. Tim had gone to sit far away from everyone else in the garden, because he wanted to start studying again. He did not want to be disturbed. The first thing to disturb him was an earwig walking across his book. The next was a dangling twig that kept coming back when he brushed it aside. He moved his position a little, and then he heard the voices:

". . . who that money really belongs to . . . his uncle's. . . ."

Tim pricked up his ears.

". . . dead twenty years . . . he was crazy."

Tim rose to his feet without a sound. He gestured to his friends at the other end of the garden.

". . . how long do you have to wait . . . stops belonging to anyone?"

Come on, this way.

"Look there," said Louis, "what is Tim doing all that pantomime for?"

Tim did not want to miss any of the conversation behind the wall, but he had to have someone with him, a witness. He could not understand it properly.

Come, come. Psst. Listen. All in sign language. Louis came running up. Quick, quick, went Tim's waving arms.

". . . would much rather Tom had it than that fellow with the yellow bike."

Who was Tom? Louis must get here at lightning speed, before Tom had William's coins.

Rumble and rattle, over the broken wall. Was that all? Two boys. But the boys were not impressed by two students. They walked calmly away, and Tim and Louis realized that there was nothing they could do about it.

"Let's not let them out of our sight. When we know where their parents live we can talk to them."

"I'll follow them," said Louis. "You tell William what you heard."

"Okay."

Louis let them turn the corner first and then went quickly in pursuit. If they had a bike somewhere, following them would be difficult. Tim ran, arms flapping, across the hot garden. The earwig was strolling over his book under the hazel tree again.

What were Alec and Chris to do now?

"Let's go and eat strawberries with Grandpa," Alec suggested. "I can hardly wait to find out what's inside the wifie, but I really don't feel like going to look at her again now."

"Okay, but we must not tell anyone else before we have really found the treasure."

"That's what I think. Tomorrow morning would be the best time to have a look. Those people at Hazelhurst Castle must not see us."

"If only we can find the place again. I think I can do it, like guessing the time, but I don't know for sure. It's more difficult in the woods than anywhere else."

"The woods are the only place where you can hide something as big as the wifie."

"Or the sea."

"Yes, but then you would never find it again. I broke some twigs to mark the way. Miss Roterdink's gravel was finished up."

"Then we're sure to find it. Hey, one of the men is following us."

"Doesn't matter. We're nearly there."

"We won't tell Grandpa anything either, eh?"

"No, nobody."

Grandpa was in the garden, pulling the yellow leaves off the tomato plants. He made light of the fact that they had stayed to eat with the Rengerinks. Alec had just time to explain to him that it had been quite impossible to refuse the invitation when the doorbell rang.

"Shall I open the door, Grandpa?"

"No, I will myself."

By the gate stood the yellow bicycle, and on the steps were William and Louis. "Good morning, sir. My name is Vandyck. I've come to see your son."

"My son?" asked Grandpa in surprise.

Louis realized their mistake. William was too excited. "We very much want to ask the two boys we saw come in here something."

"Two boys. Oh, my grandson. Of course."

They followed Grandpa along the narrow hallway, through the kitchen, and out again. There were the two boys, side by side on a seat, eating strawberries.

"Hello," said William with difficulty. He did not look friendly. "I hear that you've found something."

"Oh, no," said Chris, "it must be a mistake."

"What were you discussing behind the wall?"

"The heat, I think. Isn't that right, Alec? We thought it was pretty warm."

William thought it was pretty warm too. He had bicycled like a madman, the last stage with Louis riding pillion. Now he was getting still warmer with anger. "Do you know that those woods are mine and are no concern of yours? And what you have found there is mine too. I'm prepared to pay a reasonable reward to the finder, but if you don't cooperate I shall bring in the police. Then we shall make sure that you talk."

"The police can't make us talk," said Chris calmly.

Alec was pleased that Chris was dealing with things. It would be all right now. Then he looked at Grandpa, standing quite still by the kitchen door.

"Alec, what has happened?"

"Nothing," said Alec.

"Something certainly has happened," said William. "In the first place they broke into my house, and now. . . ."

"Is that true, Alec?"

"We only went to have a look. It was empty, wasn't it? It had been empty for twenty years, and you can just push the window up. That's not breaking in."

"I want you to tell me everything," said Grandpa softly, his voice shaking.

Excitement is not good for his heart, thought Alec suddenly. He had heard that. His mother had said so before he came here. And there was Grandpa, painfully hunched forward.

"I don't mind telling you," he said, "but they must go."

This was more than William could bear. For weeks he had searched and questioned and beaten his head against a brick wall. All the people he had talked to had kept something hidden from him. And now that the secret was close, two children were opposing him. He would bang their heads together until they cracked.

Fortunately Louis was there too. "Perhaps it would be better for us to explain everything to this gentleman first. There's no need to worry. Won't you sit down?"

Grandpa really had to sit down. He also had to take a small pill, which he had picked with shaking fingers from a little tin. Alec was feeling acutely unhappy. He would very much have liked to say or do something nice for Grandpa, but he could not. He shifted closer to Chris so that Grandpa could sit beside him on the garden seat.

Chris looked at William's nervous wriggles and thought, He'll go mad, just like his uncle. The idea gave him a guilty feeling, but he was unwilling to yield to it. They hadn't done anything wrong, had they? But spying on someone was wrong. And if Alec's grandpa was sick it was William's fault, not his and Alec's.

Grandpa was recovering a little. "It's nothing," he said. "It's passing already. It must be the heat. Let's go indoors. It's cool in there."

Shuffling very slowly, he went into the house with Alec close at his heels. The two young men and, finally, Chris followed. He would have preferred to stay with the strawberries, but if Alec was going he must go with him. Who knew what he might give away otherwise?

The curtains were drawn in the sitting room. A stray bee buzzed among the geraniums.

"Sit down, sit down," said Grandpa, lowering himself gently into his own armchair by the window. Alec stayed close to him. Louis took one of the four chairs around the table, but William was much too restless. He crossed the entire room in three strides and then took three strides back again. Chris stayed on his feet too.

"William, you explain what it's all about," said Louis. But William did not agree. The whole wretched family history—his mad uncle with the coins, the solitary aunt who had let everything go to pieces, his own desperate worries, his uncertainty about the past—might be a good story for Louis, but for him it was bitter and humiliating. And there was no need for these tiresome boys, this feeble old man to know anything about it.

He said nothing, and the only sound in the room came from the impatient bee that wanted to get out and couldn't. The silence didn't last long, but thoughts move quickly, and the tension was growing in everyone there. Grandpa, now that the pain was over, was thinking again about what William had said: that Alec had broken into his house. Alec was thinking about Grandpa's heart. A heart went *thump, thump, thump*, and if it stopped even for a moment, you were dead. Louis was thinking, I meant well, but it was obviously wrong. What shall I do? And Chris was listening to the bee. It might well be one from Janna's hives. Janna had particularly wanted to be alone today. What had she done? It would be typical of her to treat a basketful of fragrant fruit with one of her herbal mixtures, to offer it for sale at Hazelhurst Castle, and as soon as the party was drugged, to go where she liked in the rose garden. But he could more readily see her weaving her way through the woods, finding Alec's broken twigs and finally the wifie. That must not happen. Now Chris himself began to feel panicky.

William could stand it no longer. He suddenly stamped his heavy shoe on the floor so that everyone jumped.

"I've got to explain it, have I? I. I. I. They can go into my house. The whole village can make a pathway through my garden. They can chatter, chatter, chatter about Hazelhurst, about me. I know it and I feel it. We were so rich. We had horses, farms, money. And now there's only a bicycle left. I am *poor*, plucked, skinned, and boned. I have debts that I did not create. And all these farmers with their wooden heads, that dried-up fish of a housekeeper, and these pigheaded boys, they all know something. They keep their mouths tight shut, and William must explain. Explain! William is mad!"

He stamped again once or twice and stormed out of the room. They heard a click and the crash of the front door slamming.

"Sorry," said Louis, "I must go with him. I'll . . . I'll come back some time. . . ."

To explain, he had meant to say, but of course that was not possible. "Sorry."

He went hurriedly out, and when he was outside he saw that William was already on his way to the village on the yellow bicycle.

CHAPTER XXIII

Found

Grandpa opened the window a crack and urged the bee out with a newspaper.

"It seems to me," he said, "that it's up to you to explain things now."

Alec nodded, but he looked at Chris.

And Chris said, "Of course. I think we must tell you everything now."

Then, together, they told him what had happened to them, what they knew, and also what they only guessed. It was a long story.

Grandpa had no doubt that if money was found, it must go to William. There was no need to find out first exactly what was inside the big cement figure. William must do that.

"We'll have something to eat," said Grandpa. "Then you can go back to Hazelhurst Castle this evening. That young man was in a state just now. You really upset him. The sooner you put it right, the better."

"Yes," said Alec, "but Tom says it's his wifie."

"But it isn't."

"Try explaining that to him."

"Well, yes, it's sad for Tom; there's nothing we can do about that."

Louis was standing doubtfully in front of Grandpa's house. Which way should he go? To the left, running after William on his bicycle in the hope of reaching the village before the bus left? Or to the right, to Hazelhurst Castle to fetch help? He looked left, he looked right, and there was the little green car, with Bo driving it. He had been sent off to buy eggs. A quarter of an hour later they had restored William to the circle of trusted friends, who were all hanging around on the terrace because they really did think it was too hot for such heavy work as digging up treasure. And they had not come there in order to ask Farmer Slot or someone else to do it. They were very concerned over William, but they could think of nothing better to comfort him than the usual teasing: "Now we shall have to dig up the entire wood," and "Aha, here comes William the Rich."

William knew they did not mean to be unkind, yet he was within an inch of having another attack of rage. But then a heavy peal rang through the high hallways. Someone was ringing the front doorbell.

"All right, what's this, the alarm bell?"

It was Alec and Chris.

"We've come to tell you what we've found."

"That's great. Come inside. William! William! Rescue

is at hand. Here you are. This is the lord of the castle."

William was looking just as grim as on the previous occasions when they had seen him. "What did you find?"

"A statue."

William had not expected this news at all, but he was not going to show it. "How nice. Even nicer if you could also tell us where we could find it."

"In the woods. And we don't know if it's worth anything, because we didn't have time to look at it properly."

"What sort of statue is it?"

"Well, to be honest, it's really very strange. We'll show you the way. Right now if possible. But first I want to ask you something."

"Yes?"

"Will you please not break it up? And leave it where it is now, because the person who took us to it is very fond of it."

"Of course I can't promise that."

"Surely you could promise not to break it up at once?"

William thought it over. "All right, I won't break it up at once."

"Okay," said Chris, "then we can go. The shortest way is through the garden."

"Wait a minute." A girl in a bikini rushed off. "I want to come. Just putting something on."

Suddenly everyone was in a hurry. One had to find shoes, another a shirt. But William was not waiting. He strode off, and with his long legs he soon was even ahead of Alec and Chris. The first stretch of garden was a wilderness. Tall grass grew among the roses. Large areas had been flattened around the remains of the fire. Farther off stood Louis's tent.

Alec pointed to the square of cement. "Look at that!"

Chris thought at once of Janna. This was just the place where she had wanted to look. The next thing they knew, they would be going to the wifie for nothing. "Mr. Vandyck! Did you look here?"

William turned his head. "That thing? That was somewhere else before. There was nothing underneath it except a colony of woodlice. That was the first thing I pulled up. I dragged that heavy slab away and dug a deep hole."

So on they went. They climbed over the stones to leave the garden. One of the girls tore her arm on the brambles. One of the boys had to kiss it better. William strode on.

In the woods Alec had the feeling that they were being followed by a host of spirits, for the low sun cast against the tree trunks a golden glow, which was extinguished from time to time by a passing shadow and then returned with a flicker of light. The air was still very warm.

To begin with they were all laughing and talking, but gradually, as the path became more difficult to follow, the exclamations grew shorter. "A squirrel!" "Ouch!" "How pretty!" Twice they saw a big, black crow.

"Listen, is that a woodpecker?"

"Oh, no, they sound quite different."

"Then what can be tapping like that in the middle of the woods?"

They stopped in order to listen. The tapping stopped equally suddenly.

"We're nearly there," said Chris. "There is the fallen tree. We have found it quickly."

He began to climb over the thick trunk, which rested aslant on its branches. There sat the wifie in the golden sunshine, with sharp shadows on her bulging form. In front of her on the ground stood a basket he knew well and behind it the bushes were in crackling movement. Someone was passing rapidly through them, but Chris was the only one to notice. Behind him came William, who gazed, speechless. Then Alec and the others. They were not speechless.

"Ooooh."

"William, your uncle was a great artist."

A girl began to laugh uncontrollably. "That's the Queen of Porn."

Tim began to walk around the figure right away, and, just as Tom had done, he gave her a pat here and there. "Splendid," said Tim, "splendid, boys, splendid!"

Guy said, "Has she been standing here twenty years all alone, with that bottom and those tits and that unspeakably stupid face? Uncle William was ahead of his time."

"But she can't stay here. We'll have to take her to Amsterdam. This is something for the National Museum. Out in the gardens. Hordes of tourists must come and look at it."

"But I don't think it's beautiful at all," cried Barbara. "I think it's horrible."

William said nothing. He was still standing there, his black-bearded face twitching.

Alec said, "She certainly must stay here. If the treasure is inside, you can take it all, but not the statue, because it's Tom wifie and he will never have another wife."

The girl who had been laughing so hard and was just recovering began all over again.

"Well," said Chris, "there it is. You promised not to break it up. You'll have to break it a little to see what's inside, but we can patch that over later."

"She's already a little broken," said Tim. "There's a hole here. That must have been the hammering we heard. We're just in time. There are tools in that basket."

"Where is the hole? Where are the tools? Give me something, a whatsit, a hammer." William was already at the back of the figure. His hand could not pass through the hole, but Chris's could.

"I can only feel a stick."

Meanwhile, others were rummaging in the basket. Guy had found a crowbar and Tim a screwdriver.

"This is a promising hole. I'll start here."

Greta was working on the swelling back with regular hammer strokes.

"Hurrah," cried Tim, "I've broken through."

"Don't do that," cried Alec. "Its such a shame!"

Louis stood looking on soberly. "The boys are right. Stop it, all of you. You too, William. We must observe the structure. You can see roughly from the outside where you'll have the best chance of finding something without destroying the whole thing."

When Chris heard that and saw that the others were

listening, he thought everything was going to be all right after all.

"That basket belongs to Janna," he told Alec. "Would you make sure that all the things stay together? I must go to her as quickly as possible. She's going to be furious."

CHAPTER XXIV

Guilt

Chris started on the long way to Janna's house with leaden steps. What lay at the end of his walk was not going to be too pleasant. And in the woods it was wonderful. The heat of the day was over, and the animals were beginning to move about. Time and again he saw something jumping away, and in his thoughts Chris said, "You don't have to be scared of me." A young roe deer peeped over her shoulder at him. He reached the level part where broom and slender trees grew and you could see a long way. There he always saw a glow of warmth above the place where the oaks had grown over Janna's little farm. Wraiths of mist crept over the field. They did not even feel cold when he walked through them.

At last he came to the farmyard by the elder tree, which was already filled with black shadows, and the well. Chris lowered the bucket, winched it up again on the groaning chain, and drank deeply from the cold water. Delicious.

There, and of course now Janna would have heard him.

She was not in the kitchen. The kettle was still warm, but the fire in the stove had almost gone out. Where could she be? In one of the small rooms with whitewashed walls and smooth tiled floors? In the dark threshing floor? No, he could see a light under the door to the big kitchen, and he could hear a rumbling sound. What was that? Softly Chris pushed the door open. It was cold in there, an oil lamp burned low on the table, and Janna sat spinning. She tramped rapidly on a small board under the spinning wheel. The wooden wheel turned, grumbling. Chris had never seen her spinning before. Her quick little hands plucked at the fleecy wool, and a strong, thin thread grew around a big bobbin. He thought it was wonderful.

Janna did not look up, and when he had been standing there for a while, she said, "Go away."

"How far do I have to go?" asked Chris.

"Go and fetch wood and stoke up the fire. There is a tall glass jar at the back of the top shelf in the closet. There are some purple-brown leaves in it. Make some tea with them."

"Okay."

Relieved, Chris went to the kitchen. If he had to go no farther than here, that was not too bad. He did everything she had told him. The tea was purple-brown as well and had a sharp scent. When it was ready, the humming drone ceased and the wooden chair legs screeched over the stones. Janna appeared in the door opening, gazing at him with her glittering black eyes, her hands on her hips.

"Is the tea ready? Have you tried it? I suppose you think it's delicious, don't you? Well, it isn't. It's the most evil-tasting, disgusting tea you can make, and it is only good for someone whose guts have gone completely wrong. I think that my guts are soon going to go completely wrong, because things have happened that I cannot bear."

She stopped in order to draw breath. Chris said nothing.

"You don't want to know, do you? It doesn't matter to you what Janna can bear, but I shall tell you all the same.

"I can't allow young William to become as rich as old William was. And I can't allow the fact that you showed that thing to him and not to me. But what I can't allow at all is that you were the first to find it and not me. And you don't even want it for yourself.

"Everyone has been looking for it, the people from Hazelhurst Castle, you and your friends, and I. When things are like that, nothing can stay hidden. Why did you have the most power? After all, you are here to learn from me how to use it. All my life I have used it just the way the women who lived here before me did. This is a living place. But you come from a hard city, and you have power on your own. I can't bear it!"

"Shall I pour you a cup of tea?"

"No, I know how it tastes. I don't want it. When William didn't need me anymore, I couldn't bear it either. My mother gave me wild tea. My power returned, and I was able to make sure that William never had another woman. How could I know that he had so little power that it sent him mad? He didn't need to go mad. A spell can drop off you like a dry leaf. That was what happened to my grief. I traveled for years and never gave him another thought. But I came back, and he had allowed it to grow up inside him until it was as big as that whale of a woman in the woods. He didn't have to let it grow. He had enough other things to think of. He had enough of everything. Except power. Or the will to shake it off. I didn't want to do him that much harm. So why have I had to bear such great guilt all my life?"

"Oh, Janna," said Chris.

"Silence. I haven't finished yet. I have said it all because I had to say it, but I can't allow you to know it. That's what the tea is for. When you swallow it, it tastes bitter and sharp. It burns in your stomach. But when it is in your gut, it will twist it and shrivel it until it is as small as a mouse's gut. There is enough for the two of us."

"I don't think a mouse's gut is big enough for me."

"You don't, eh? Hee-hee-hee-hee-hee."

Janna took two mugs and a spoon. "We'll put some honey in it. It won't stop it from working."

Chris thought, Poor Janna, what am I to do about this? Then he thought, I'm not scared. How is it that I'm never scared?

Janna poured the tea and went on stirring the honey into it, on and on. Was it really poison? Perhaps she was just pretending.

"Where are the scissors? I promised to make a doll from your hair. Surely I could do that first?"

"If you are no longer here, there doesn't have to be a doll."

"Oh, no, that's true."

She looked straight at him, her eyes strange. "You're not afraid. How is it that you're not afraid?"

"I don't know."

"Here is your tea."

Chris accepted the cup, thinking, She's pretending. One swallow can surely do no harm. Janna watched and watched. She saw that he was really going to drink. Then the tears sprang into her eyes, and she began to weep desperately. Chris picked up the teapot at once, took it outside, and poured the tea out over the stones. He threw the teacups out too, in a wide arc.

"Come on, Janna, come outside."

The moon had risen, there were gnats in the air, small bats with transparent wings, and dark owls. One of the cats was sitting on the edge of the well.

Chris said, "I think this is the most beautiful place in the world. And the powers are not ours but the earth's. You taught me that yourself."

"Yes, that is true. And the moon's, too. To be able to work with powers, you have to let everything else go. I know how it is, you see." She dried her tears with a corner of her blue apron.

They sat silently side by side in the night and saw the stars appearing. Then Janna said, "I have let it go. It is even more difficult to let grief go than anything else. You don't know that because you're still young. You haven't experienced anything yet. But later on, one day, you'll remember."

"Yes," said Chris, "later I shall remember."

CHAPTER XXV

Money

They looked at the structure. The base was roughly square. Chris had felt one stick. There were probably four sticks, meeting at the top, with heavy wire netting laid over them in the shape of a seated woman. Everything had been plastered with cement and heavily thickened in many places. The head had been added on top.

"The best thing would be to open the back up some more, but toward the middle. The back is fairly straight."

William wanted to do it himself, with crowbar and hammer. The cement cracked but stayed hanging on the wire, until suddenly a big piece tore away and fell inward. Now you could see the four stakes and a fifth in the middle, resting on wood.

"Oh," cried William, "that's the coin chest. He showed it to me long ago when I was here." He tugged at the raw edges of the masonry.

"A much bigger piece will have to come out. It's a sizable chest."

After a while the wifie had no back left, but the chest could not be got out until part of the side had suffered too. Alec stood looking on sadly. There was really nothing he could do.

The chest that finally appeared had once been very beautiful. There were carved flowers on the uprights, but it was covered with gray and green mold, and the veneer had peeled away and hung in tatters. There were ten drawers.

William was able to open one of them with difficulty. The jerk sent a couple of big golden coins rolling on the ground. Everyone wanted to see.

"That is a rose noble," said Guy. "I've seen one of them. It cost four thousand guilders."

The whole drawer was filled with coins similar to the rose noble, set neatly on edge like chocolates in a slot into which they fitted precisely. William managed to open one drawer after another. In the lowest drawer everything lay higgledy-piggledy, gold and silver together. In the top one there were cigarette cases.

"I recognize them all now that I see them," said William. "In here he had forgeries, coins on which, for one reason or another, the year or something else had been changed. These are rare, and these are the rarest of all. There should be one here with an Egyptian hieroglyph on it. There are only two of them left in the world. And here is Alexander the Great's campaign. Tetra drachmae from all the places he conquered."

His friends stood looking on, rather surprised. William seemed to have turned into quite a different person, as he

displayed all the gold to them. The sky grew dark, but you could still see the shining yellow pieces quite well.

"Well, well!" said Louis. "So? What shall we do with them?"

"I shall sell most of them," said William.

"Are you going to invite your customers here, in the woods?"

"Oh . . . yes . . . perhaps you could go and borrow a wheelbarrow from Slot. I would rather not leave them."

"You're not going to get a wheelbarrow through these woods."

"Perhaps we could reach it another way. This thing wasn't made here, after all. It must have been brought on a cart at one time."

"Yes, and afterward all these trees were planted. Have you seen how much ivy is growing everywhere? The intention was that this female should never be found."

"We shall just have to come back tomorrow with all the boxes and rucksacks we can find. It's too dark now. We're sure to get lost."

"I'm staying here."

"But William, you can't stay through the night."

"It's not cold."

"This is the warmest night for the last hundred years," said Louis. "I would like to stay too."

"No, Louis," said Greta, "there are sure to be wild pigs."

"Tom may come," said Alec, "and if he sees that his wifie has been broken, he might be a lot more dangerous than a wild pig. He is very strong."

They went on debating the point. Then Louis said, "You must go. It's getting darker and darker. William doesn't want to leave. I can understand that, and I shall keep him company. But there won't be much question of sleeping, without blankets, so we would appreciate it if you could be here early tomorrow morning with boxes and bags. Off you go now. Alec, can you still remember the way?"

"I hope so," said Alec. He went stoutly ahead, and one by one William's friends followed him into the darkness of the woods, their footsteps rustling.

"I'm going to look for bracken," said Louis. "It's big and springy, and it's the best thing to lie on or under, if we do want to sleep a bit."

"Okay," said William absently, but he didn't go with Louis. Sleep was the last thing he was thinking about. He opened the topmost drawer again. Was that little Egyptian coin still there? How much would that tiny thing be worth now? And the rest of them? He sat on one knee of the wifie, who began to look like a threatening divinity in the darkness. He began to add up figures.

He was rich now, but he would have to spend a lot. First, of course, a present for the boys who had led him here. What should he give them? A bike or something? And he must take his friends out to dinner. And whatever else he did, he must buy new shoes, of soft leather, and at least one size bigger. He would keep part of the capital so that he would be able to buy good shoes all his life.

"William," said Louis, "here's a lovely bed for you.

Come and sleep a bit now, before nightfall brings the dew and makes it impossible. We may have to run about to keep warm."

Fair enough. William snuggled down between the giant ferns that Louis had gathered. It was true; he was as comfortable as in a bed. Louis, beside him, was asleep in no time, but William was still wakeful. He saw the moon rising, and he was occupied with his thoughts.

What was he to do with the castle? Have it restored? Make a nice warm house of it, with a neat garden? Bring the old paintings back to the broad corridor, Aunt Reine's dark, gleaming furniture in the high rooms, and roses, roses all along the paths?

Of course it was there, by the roses, that the figure had originally stood. At last William realized what had happened in the past and why Slot and Miss Roterdink had been so strangely silent. They had cared for Uncle William for years, protected him, while he behaved more and more oddly and said strange things. But it was too much when he made that monstrous thing, which stood outside where everyone could see it. Uncle William was taken away, and the figure too. It must have been tremendously hard work to make it. They had watched him toiling at it, and because they were still fond of him despite his madness, they did not want to break it up. Perhaps they thought he might be back one day.

They probably did not know that the precious collection was inside. Slot had realized now, of course, when the search was on, but he had already said that he knew nothing about it. Although things were no longer as bad as they would have been twenty years ago, it was possible that they still had difficulty in accepting that the baron had made such a shaming thing, especially the old spinster. Would it be better for the wifie to be broken up after all? Would he have to sell the house? Travel, never come back, and forget it all? Uncle William, would he ever understand him?

Louis turned over. William heard something in the wood. Wild pig, after all?

"Louis, Louis, listen. What's that?"

"Hmmm," said Louis. "A rabbit."

"No, it must be much bigger." William sat up. He tried to see if there was anything there, by the bushes where the moon shed a gray light. He heard no more.

Louis fell asleep again. William stayed awake. He stared at the huge sky, at the glittering stars: ducats and doubloons.

Alec had no built-in signpost like Chris, and under the dark trees he could no longer see which way they had come. The moment soon came when he did not know where he was, but he did not show it. He walked on at random and sooner than he had expected he recognized the path he had walked along that afternoon with Chris, when they were trying out the ram's horn. What a long time ago it seemed.

At last they reached the castle. Saskia took him home in the little green car.

Grandpa already had the night bolt on the door. "I'm glad you're here. I was getting anxious. Did it go well?"

"Yes," said Alec, "there really was a treasure in the wifie: a chest full of gold coins."

"You must tell me everything tomorrow. It's too late now. Would you like some hot chocolate?"

Hot chocolate on a day like this? What made Grandpa think of that? Oh, well, actually he would like some.

"You go straight upstairs. It will be ready in a minute, and I'll bring it up."

When Alec reached his hot little room, he was glad he had not come home sooner. The sun had been shining on the sloping roof all day. He pushed his blanket off at once and lay tossing and turning.

He might just as well have stayed up talking to Grandpa, because he could not help thinking of all the things they had done that day and he could not go to sleep. Finally he began doing figures. One of the coins cost over four thousand guilders and that was not even a very special one, because the most costly of all were in a separate part of the chest, at least thirty or forty of them. How much could they be worth? Surely at least five thousand guilders each. That made at least a hundred and fifty thousand. And how many coins were there altogether in the ten drawers? Ten times a hundred? No, many more. More than a thousand coins altogether. A thousand times a thousand. That William had become very rich indeed all at once. Would he give him and Chris anything? Or Tom?

Queer that Tom had arrived just as they were blowing

on the ram's horn. And he had taken them to the treasure, too. But Tom was no spirit, so they had not made magic. Or had they? The time really had come for him to think everything over properly at last.

It was much too hot in bed. Alec went to sit by the window and looked out. On the roof of the shed he could see that the moon was shining, but it was on the other side of the house. How different it looked from the daytime. Everything was gray and spooky. The last time he had sat looking out here, he had been reading about appearances in Grandpa's book. The idea appealed to him less now. And when the night was dark there was no appearance at all. The book told you all about making magic. Chris believed it, but he did not want to talk about it. Grandpa believed it too, but Grandpa was a bit nutty. He would never get any more from him. He kept on harping about the book and was scared of it at the same time. He read about rottentooth but had never looked for it. If Alec wanted to know anything about magic, he would have to read the book himself.

The whole thing was certainly an awful nuisance, but now he did want to know. By learning the strange language? Oh, perhaps that wouldn't be necessary. For the time being, great-great-grandfather Alec Aulder's book was difficult enough. He must get his hands on that first. Then he would find out exactly what it said about the ram's horn. It was a coincidence that Tom had led them to the wifie, an extraordinary coincidence.

Alec went back to bed. He did not stay at the window

long enough to see that it was to be a night ablaze with stars.

Tom saw the stars. He wandered through the wood with his ram's horn. They had sent him away again.

"Be off, go and blow somewhere else," his sister had told him. Tom's patience was endless. He was practicing to make exactly the same sound as the boy had made, but at home they did not want to hear it. When he was sent away he stopped blowing. After all, he could do it by now, and he was feeling a little sulky. It was difficult and he had learned it. At last he had learned something difficult, and no one thought it was bright of him. "Be off, go and blow somewhere else." They did not want him. Tom wandered among the trees in the pale moonlight, on and on. Where was he going? To the wifie, of course. His own, delicious, fat wifie had never sent him packing. There he always found comfort, when he could not understand other people.

Tom was a strong, heavy man, but he made very little noise. A twig snapped from time to time or a bush rustled, but he stepped as softly on the ground as the animals that lived there, because he was accustomed to the silence of nature.

When he climbed over the fallen tree, he saw something unusual right away: the coin chest. He did not examine it closely, nor did he notice that there were two men lying on the ground nearby. Something was wrong. What had happened to his wifie? The broad, flat, noseless face was as familiar to him by night as by day. She looked at him as she always did. Only when he walked around the figure did he see the great wound in her side. Her splendid behind had gone. To his horror Tom found himself looking into a deep, black hole. Unable to bear it, he went away.

He wandered around in confusion and went on wandering. He thought of nothing, for in his head there was little room for thoughts and it was filled with sorrow.

At last he came to an open place where five oak trees grew. There he was able to think again. A memory arose in him of the ram's horn. He must not blow it here, the boys had told him.

They had destroyed his wifie.

Tom took the ram's horn from his pocket and began to blow.

He could do it. He knew exactly how it should sound. He could do it better, louder. He blew with all the power he had in him, and he felt himself no longer sad, but mighty. Tom, the great horn blower. His voice reached up to the stars.